CRAZY ADULT FACTS THAT SOUND COMPLETELY MADE UP

A FUN FACTS BOOK FOR ADULTS WHO APPRECIATE THE UNEXPECTED SIDE OF TRIVIA

MILLIE MOORE

Copyright © 2025 Millie Moore

All rights reserved. No part of this publication may be reproduced, distributed or transmitted in any form or by any means, including photocopying, recording, or other electronic or mechanical methods, without the prior written permission of the publisher, except in the case of brief quotations embodied in critical reviews and certain other non-commercial uses permitted by copyright law.

Trademarked names appear throughout this book. Rather than use a trademark symbol with every occurrence of a trademarked name, names are used in an editorial fashion, with no intention of infringement of the respective owner's trademark. The information in this book is distributed on an "as is" basis, without warranty. Although every precaution has been taken in the preparation of this work, neither the author nor the publisher shall have any liability to any person or entity with respect to any loss or damage caused or alleged to be caused directly or indirectly by the information contained in this book.

CONTENTS

1. Love, Lust & the Weird Side of Sex — 1
2. Adult Icons & Provocative Fame — 9
3. Savage Nature & Shocking Wildlife — 18
4. Crazy Creations & Accidental Inventions — 27
5. Weird Science & Cosmic Oddities — 36
6. Ghosts, Magic & Creepy Rituals — 46
7. Viral Madness & Online Insanity — 58
8. Freakish Bodies & Medical Nightmares — 69
9. Hidden Scandals & Star Confessions — 77
10. Absurd Laws & Political Blunders — 89
11. Dark Laughs & Bizarre Headlines — 99
12. Murderous Minds & Cult Horrors — 108
13. Secrets, Lies & Collective Madness — 122
14. Strange Events & Gruesome Fates — 133
15. Substances, Trips & Party Chaos — 146
16. Atrocities, Brutality & Dark Warfare — 155
17. Mysterious Rites & Ancient Customs — 166

1. Love, Lust & the Weird Side of Sex

Sex blends biology, psychology, and curiosity. Research uncovers the strange, fascinating, and often misunderstood aspects of love, lust, and sexual behavior.

1. Hard, fast thrusting may feel intense, but for many women it can cause discomfort or even small injuries. The skin near the vaginal opening is especially sensitive, making gentler movements safer and often more enjoyable.

2. Men can train themselves to separate orgasm from ejaculation, since the two are controlled by different physiological processes. With practice, it's possible to experience orgasmic pleasure without releasing semen, a technique sometimes linked to tantric or prolonged sexual practices.

3. Although it's often said you should avoid intimacy with an ex, breakup sex can sometimes have the opposite effect. A 2018 study suggests that sleeping with an ex may actually help some people find closure and move on emotionally. For others, though, it can prolong attachment — so its impact really depends on the individual.

4. In surveys exploring political differences and sexuality, researchers found that Republicans were more likely than Democrats to report fantasies involving taboo or "immoral" themes. These included scenarios that broke social or cultural rules, such as infidelity or power dynamics.

5. Research shows that a healthy sex life doesn't just boost mood at home — it can also improve job satisfaction and work performance. Regular intimacy is linked to lower stress, higher energy, and better overall focus during the workday.

6. The pullout method is unreliable because even the semen released before ejaculation can contain sperm capable of causing pregnancy. This means that relying on withdrawal alone carries a significant risk of unintended conception.

7. Low sex drive isn't just a women's issue — men can experience it too. In fact, many couples deal with mismatched levels of desire, no matter

their gender. These differences are common and often shift with stress, health, or life changes, making open communication an important part of navigating them.

8. Sexual fantasies are nearly universal, but not quite. A 2025 study shows that about 3% of people report never having any sexual fantasies at all. This makes them a small minority in a world where most minds wander toward erotic imagination at some point.

9. Unlike medical devices, sex toys aren't closely regulated, which means some may be made from materials that aren't body-safe. Because of this, experts recommend choosing products from reputable brands or retailers that clearly list their materials. Buying carefully helps ensure both safety and peace of mind.

10. Desire and arousal don't always follow the same script. For many people, sexual interest builds only after physical or emotional stimulation, rather than sparking beforehand. This is sometimes called responsive desire, and it's just as normal as feeling "in the mood" right away.

11. Using cucumbers or other household objects during sex may seem harmless, but it can actually be risky. These items aren't made for the body, so they can splinter, break, or carry harmful bacteria. For safety and comfort, it's best to stick to toys made from body-safe materials designed for intimate use.

12. A 2021–2022 study found that many sexual fantasies often turn into action, with about half of them being tried at least once, with bondage, discipline, sadism, and masochism showing one of the strongest matches. Sharing fantasies is common too: a 2025 review linked fantasy talk to better communication, and newer surveys put sharing at nearly 70%, usually with positive experiences. Bottom line: almost everyone has fantasies (around 90–97%), and many use them intentionally to boost desire.

13. When men rely heavily on a very specific style of masturbation, it can sometimes make partnered sex feel less satisfying because their bodies may become conditioned to respond best to that exact stimulation. As a result, adjusting to a partner's touch can be more challenging until habits shift.

14. A 2024 study shows that sexting (sending sexually explicit messages or images) can strengthen intimacy for couples, often leading to greater sexual and relationship satisfaction. For singles, though, the benefits aren't as clear — sexting may be exciting, but it doesn't consistently boost overall well-being. The impact seems to depend on whether there is an ongoing, committed connection behind the messages.

15. Women can have multiple orgasms, but many don't explore this potential due to a lack of information or support.

16. Great sex isn't only about penetration — it's about the whole spectrum of intimacy. Touch, kissing, oral sex, and emotional closeness all play just as big a role. Focusing on these different forms of connection often leads to a more fulfilling sexual experience for both partners.

17. Dyspareunia refers to persistent pain during intercourse and can affect both men and women, often stemming from physical, medical, or psychological causes.

18. Getting older doesn't mean giving up on a fulfilling sex life. Many older adults report satisfying intimacy, often enriched by greater confidence, emotional closeness, and open communication. In fact, experience can make sexual relationships deeper and more rewarding over time.

19. Pelvic inflammatory disease is a serious infection that usually develops when sexually transmitted infections like chlamydia or gonorrhea go untreated. It can cause deep pelvic pain, along with fever or unusual discharge, and may lead to lasting complications such as infertility or chronic pain. Early testing and treatment are key to preventing long-term damage.

20. It's rare for two people to want sex at the exact same frequency or intensity all the time. Most couples discover that their libidos don't perfectly align, and they need to navigate those differences with patience and communication. Over time, negotiating desire becomes a natural part of building intimacy.

21. Erectile dysfunction may be an early warning sign of coronary artery disease due to reduced blood flow and should prompt a medical evaluation.

22. A 2018 survey shows that group sex tops the list of fantasies for many Americans. Right behind it are themes like BDSM and other taboo scenarios, which often appeal because they break social norms. While not everyone wants to act them out, these fantasies are among the most frequently reported.

23. Many sexually transmitted diseases don't show any obvious symptoms, which means a person can carry an infection without ever realizing it. Feeling healthy or looking clean isn't enough to guarantee safety because hygiene by itself cannot prevent or reveal an STD. That's why regular testing is so important — it's the only reliable way to detect infections early and stop them from spreading. Just as vital is open and honest communication with your partner, since trust and testing together create the foundation for real sexual health.

24. A sense of humor during sex can make the experience more enjoyable and reduce anxiety over imperfections.

25. Arousal fluid occurs when the body senses sexual desire or attraction. During this process, there is increased blood flow to the genitals, including the vaginal walls, which causes fluid to pass through them, making the tissues wet and providing lubrication.

26. About 1 in 6 women say they have never experienced an orgasm. Still, that doesn't mean sex can't be enjoyable — intimacy, touch, and emotional connection can provide plenty of satisfaction on their own. For many, pleasure goes far beyond just reaching climax.

27. A burning or itchy sensation in the vagina is often a sign of infection, but the cause can vary. Yeast infections and bacterial vaginosis are two of the most common culprits, and while their symptoms may overlap, they need different treatments. That's why getting a proper diagnosis before starting medication is so important.

28. Sexual satisfaction isn't all about the finish line. Many people find intimacy fulfilling through touch, connection, and pleasure, even without an orgasm. In fact, putting too much pressure on climax can create stress and actually make the experience less enjoyable.

29. In ancient Greece, prostitutes wore sandals that imprinted "Follow Me" into the dirt.

30. It's possible for food allergies to cause problems even in the bedroom. If someone with a severe Brazil nut allergy has sex with a partner who recently ate them, traces of the allergen can be passed through saliva or other bodily fluids, which can trigger a reaction, making communication and caution especially important in such cases.

31. Vestibulodynia is a condition where the entrance of the vagina feels painful or burning, often during initial penetration or even light touch. Because the symptoms can overlap with other issues, it usually requires a careful and thorough medical evaluation to diagnose correctly. With the right treatment, many women are able to manage the pain and improve comfort over time.

32. What plays out in the mind or on a screen doesn't always work the same way in reality. Sexual fantasies can be exciting to imagine, but they often don't translate smoothly into practice. Porn can add to the gap by setting unrealistic expectations about bodies, stamina, and how sex "should" look.

33. A man's arousal can't be measured by an erection alone. Desire often shows up in other ways — through touch, emotion, or simply wanting closeness. That's why open communication and embracing the full-body experience matter more than relying on one physical signal.

34. Studies show condoms don't reduce women's sexual pleasure.

35. Cold water can rinse away sperm more effectively than warm or hot water, since heat may cause proteins in semen to coagulate and stick. Interestingly, some ancient cultures believed that washing immediately after sex could prevent pregnancy, though modern science proves it's not enough. And while rinsing can remove surface semen, it won't protect against STDs, so using proper protection is still key.

36. Premature ejaculation is usually defined as climaxing right before or shortly after penetration, often leaving little time for satisfaction. While it's a common concern, many men who worry about finishing "too soon" are actually within the normal range of sexual timing—usually between 3 and

7 minutes of intercourse. What matters most is whether it causes distress for the individual or couple.

37. The most effective tool for better sex isn't a gadget or a trick — it's communication. Letting your partner know what feels good and what doesn't builds trust, deepens connection, and makes intimacy more satisfying for both of you. In the end, honest conversation often leads to the most memorable experiences.

38. 12% of adults admit to having sex at their workplace at least once.

39. Genital warts are a common STI caused by certain strains of HPV, and they sometimes go unnoticed because they may be small or hidden. While the warts themselves aren't life-threatening, the virus is linked to more serious risks if left unchecked, including cervical, anal, and even oral cancers. Regular checkups and vaccinations are key to prevention and early detection.

40. Sex therapy offers support for a wide range of concerns, from performance anxiety and mismatched desire to physical challenges like pain or difficulty with arousal. By combining open conversation with practical strategies, therapists help individuals and couples explore solutions in a safe space. For many, it's a path toward greater confidence, intimacy, and satisfaction.

41. Surveys show women who play video games have more sex and happier relationships than those who don't.

42. Vaginal dryness often shows up during breastfeeding, menopause, or as a side effect of certain medications. It can make sex uncomfortable, but lubricants are a simple way to ease the irritation. Many people prefer organic options, since they're free of harsh chemicals and gentler on sensitive tissue.

43. Persistent genital arousal disorder causes unwanted and repeated arousal in women, which can be distressing and painful without medical intervention.

44. Sex isn't only about pleasure; it can leave measurable fingerprints on your health. During arousal and orgasm, heart rate and circulation rise like a brief workout, and over time, regular intimacy has been linked to

better cardiovascular markers and lower blood pressure. Hormones shift too: oxytocin and endorphins counter stress, prolactin and melatonin nudge sleep, and testosterone/estrogen fluctuations can support libido, mood, and even bone health. There's an immune angle as well — frequent, satisfying sex is associated with higher levels of certain antibodies, suggesting your body may get a small defense boost alongside the afterglow.

The mental spillover is just as real. Touch and closeness reduce cortisol, ease anxiety, and can improve pain tolerance and mood, making intimacy feel like a built-in stress intervention. It's not a miracle cure — quality, consent, and safety matter far more than a tally — but when sex is wanted, comfortable, and protected, it often acts like a compact wellness practice for body and mind.

45. Ejaculation travels at an average speed of 11 miles per hour (18 kilometers per hour).

46. Endometriosis, a condition where tissue similar to the uterine lining grows outside the uterus, can cause deep pelvic pain during sex, often making intimacy uncomfortable or even distressing. It's also one of the more difficult conditions to diagnose, sometimes taking years of medical visits before being identified. Roughly 1 in 9 women — about 11% — are affected, highlighting just how common yet underrecognized it is.

47. Deep penetration sometimes leads to discomfort if the cervix is bumped, which can be more noticeable in certain positions or around menstruation, when the cervix tends to be lower and more sensitive. Adjusting angles or trying different positions often helps reduce the pressure and make sex more comfortable.

48. Lifelong singles have a 42% higher risk of developing dementia, and widowers also face increased health risks.

49. In controlled settings, romantic partners' heart rates and breathing synchronize simply by sitting together and gazing silently. Strangers don't show the effect. Some studies find women's physiology more often adjusts to match partners, reflecting subtle interpersonal regulation.

50. Silicone-based lubricants can ease dryness and reduce discomfort during sex, and reducing antihistamine use may help too, since these medications can cause vaginal dryness. Still, if pain persists, it's important to see a specialist to rule out underlying conditions and find tailored treatment. Professional guidance ensures the problem isn't just managed but properly addressed.

2. Adult Icons & Provocative Fame

From money shots to hidden dangers, the adult industry shapes fantasies and culture alike, blending scandal, secrecy, and surprising truths.

51. The "money shot" is still treated as a required deliverable in many productions. If a male performer can't complete on camera, it can cost him the day's paycheck. To avoid losing a scene, studios may occasionally bring in a stand-in for a close-up, then edit the footage seamlessly so the substitution isn't visible to viewers.

52. Not every thrust you see is real contact; camera framing can hide inches of air. In doggy-style with a rear three-quarter angle, a flaccid penis can be visible even as the hips slap for sound and motion.

53. Surveys show that 20% of men admit to watching pornography online while at work, compared to about 13% of women.

54. Porn and child exploitation can overlap in disturbing ways — especially when images or videos of minors end up on mainstream sites. That can happen through grooming, coercion, hacking, trafficking, or even so-called "revenge porn." In recent years, big platforms have faced lawsuits claiming they hosted or made money off this kind of content before taking it down. Even with bans in place, moderation isn't perfect — some material slips through or gets re-uploaded again and again. The hard truth is that even a private viewing habit can feed demand, creating an incentive for people to post abusive content.

55. In August 2012, the Los Angeles adult film industry shut down for several weeks after veteran porn star Jesse "Mr. Marcus" Spencer continued filming despite testing positive for syphilis — he falsified test results to conceal his infection. He later pleaded no contest and received a 30-day jail sentence, along with probation and community service, for knowingly exposing co-stars to the disease.

56. A Harvard study found that online porn subscriptions are higher in conservative states.

57. Veteran performers keep "no-list" spreadsheets of people they won't work with, with reasons attached. Common flags include STI status, roughness beyond consent, racist ad-libs, premature finishing, substance use, or boundary pushing — like uncalled-for anal.

58. While 25% to 33% of those who watch Internet porn are women, they make up only 2% of paying porn site subscribers.

59. Porn can train viewers to see others as instruments for personal gratification rather than full people, a process called sexual objectification. Research in 2024 and 2025 links objectification to greater acceptance of a range of sexual harms. Scripts that reward conquest, novelty, and performance can bleed into everyday expectations with partners. The more those scripts are rehearsed, the more they can shape attitudes and behavior.

60. The docu-series *Family Business*, which centers on director and performer Seymour Butts, offers an unusually candid look at budgets, casting, and family fallout. Though dated, it remains useful for separating fantasy from workflow. Behind the scenes, it's more logistics than lust.

61. Disney renamed the film *Moana* to *Oceana* in Italy to avoid association with Moana Pozzi, a famous Italian adult film star.

62. Bonnie Blue's reported income of $1 to 2 million per month — estimated at over $40 million annually — placed her among the most profitable independent creators worldwide. Her earnings rivaled or surpassed those of well-known figures such as Riley Reid and Lana Rhoades.

63. In North Korea and Iran, producing or distributing pornography is a capital offense, punishable by death. Both countries enforce some of the harshest anti-pornography laws in the world.

64. After President Bush won the election in 2004, Republican states saw a jump in porn-related Internet searches. After President Obama won, blue states saw a jump in Internet searches. Researchers suggest that being on a winning team creates a surge of testosterone, which increases sex drive.

65. According to a 2024 report, California ranks highest among U.S. states for overall porn engagement, and among Californians, "animated"

is said to be one of the most popular categories. Washington reportedly logs the most porn-related searches per person. However, emerging age-verification laws and website blocks make raw traffic numbers harder to interpret accurately—these rankings are better seen as approximate signals rather than exact measurements.

66. The word "pornography" first appeared in the Oxford English Dictionary in 1857.

67. Many actors report preferring plain, affectionate sex off-camera and experiencing low libido off-set due to burnout. Dating can be difficult when partners assume that on-screen preferences reflect real-life desires. For some, regular sex drops to nearly zero between shoots.

68. Although strongly associated with adult entertainment, OnlyFans also hosts chefs, musicians, comedians, and fitness instructors, giving creators control over pricing, content, and boundaries.

69. In Japan, female performers vastly outnumber male talent, creating a chronic shortage of men on set. As a result, the same handful of male actors appear across thousands of titles. It's a supply-and-demand quirk that shapes what you see on screen.

70. There are public "death databases" that track adult performer passings by cause. When you scroll through them, you'll see suicides, overdoses — and, more than many expect, homicides — among the entries. They're imperfect records, but they paint a sobering picture of risk and instability.

71. The average porn site visit lasts 6 minutes and 20 seconds.

72. In 2001, hackers took over a display screen in a Dresden, Germany, supermarket and replaced its daily specials with a live sex channel. Shoppers were stunned as explicit content played on the store's big screen.

73. Estimates suggest the global pornography industry generates around $100 billion annually, making it larger than the combined revenues of all professional basketball, baseball, and football franchises. Porn revenue has also been reported to exceed the combined yearly earnings of major U.S. networks like ABC, CBS, and NBC, which total about $6.2 billion.

74. The earliest surviving American film showing intercourse is known today by the title *A Grass Sandwich* and was shot in New Jersey in 1915.

75. A 2024 study found that watching porn did increase hostile sexist attitudes, but only in people who already had those tendencies. These tendencies include higher antagonism, unfriendliness, suspiciousness, and disagreeability.

76. Many performers supplement their income by touring strip clubs for feature dances and meet-and-greets. Names like Lisa Ann, Jenna Haze, and Teagan Presley built substantial earnings this way. It's part marketing, part livelihood hedge.

77. More performers than you'd think have college degrees — and some even have advanced ones. People get into the industry for all kinds of reasons: money, flexible hours, curiosity — not just because they're out of options. Having a degree doesn't protect anyone from the risks, but it does push back against the usual stereotypes about who ends up in the business and why.

78. In Normandy, France, a preschool teacher thought she was clicking on a cartoon when she inadvertently clicked on a hardcore porn file. Not realizing her mistake, she left the room before the clip began, and the film played for several minutes.

79. CGI and automated dialogue replacement — including pre-recorded moans — are more common in adult films than many realize. On-set audio often includes unglamorous elements like grunts, technical instructions, and background noise — such as camera rigs or fans. To create a more polished and erotic experience, many of the sounds are added in post-production, shaping the illusion of passion through editing.

80. While viewing porn, men tend to focus on a woman's eyes and lips over breasts or genitals. Researchers speculate that men look at women's faces to determine how "turned on" the woman is.

81. Johnny Sins, whose real name is Steven Wolfe, represents the opposite image — a modern, meme-friendly version of adult fame. Known for his shaved head, muscular build, and friendly persona, he became an internet icon not just for his work in adult films but for the sheer range of "profes-

sions" he played on camera — from doctor and firefighter to astronaut and teacher. This running joke turned him into a global meme symbolizing versatility and humor in adult entertainment. After retiring from mainstream filming, Johnny Sins built a strong online presence as a fitness and lifestyle influencer, turning adult notoriety into mainstream relatability. His career reflects the new generation of performers who manage their image like brands — approachable, self-aware, and internet-savvy.

82. Porn was mistakenly aired for an entire 10 minutes in the background during a national TV news report on Syria in January 2013 on Sweden's TV4 network.

83. A 2023 study from the Netherlands found only a small link between pornography use and sexual experience, including behaviors like paying for sex, one-night stands, or adventurous sexual practices. The findings suggest porn consumption has little impact on most people's real-world sexual behavior.

84. Deep-throat and aggressive face scenes may involve topical anesthetics that numb the gag reflex and reduce irritation. Sprays used for cough suppression can also act as mild antiseptics. "Training" is real, but chemical help is common on extreme sets.

85. At the height of her notoriety, Bonnie Blue's Wikipedia page reportedly attracted more visitors than Beyoncé's. This unusual surge in traffic underscored her global visibility and showed how viral stunts in adult entertainment can capture mainstream attention, turning digital spectacle into worldwide fascination.

86. The Hong Kong film *3-D Sex and Zen: Extreme Ecstasy*, produced for $3.2 million, was marketed as the world's first 3D pornographic movie. Released in 2011, it became a box office sensation in parts of Asia.

87. Heavy or coping-driven porn use is associated in studies with higher loneliness, more anxiety and depressive symptoms, lower life satisfaction, and poorer self-esteem. The relationship can run both ways: people who feel isolated may watch more, and watching more can deepen isolation and secrecy. Hiding a behavior from loved ones often erodes closeness, which can further harm mental health. Many report improved well-being after reducing or quitting.

88. Adult entertainment has been an early, aggressive adopter of consumer tech: VHS, streaming, paywalls, DRM, and subscription models. When the industry leans into a format, it's often a leading indicator of mainstream viability. When it ignores one, like consumer VR, growth can stall.

89. Before her death, Dakota Skye claimed some shoots paid a "jailbait bonus" for women who appeared underage — those with a petite build, small breasts, minimal tattoos, and even braces. The allegation highlights how "barely legal" aesthetics monetize youthfulness. It's a controversy that won't go away.

90. That dramatic bounce that seems to defy gravity isn't always physics. Sometimes, a personal assistant out of frame is pulling wrists or ankles to create extra motion. Camera angles hide the assist while selling "natural" physics.

91. Clitoral atrophy befalls a woman who doesn't have sex for long periods. This medical condition comes in the form of a loss of sexual sensation. The clitoris withdraws into the body when it's not receiving enough blood flow. On the other hand, males also experience penile atrophy due to injury or aging.

92. During the COVID-19 lockdowns, OnlyFans experienced explosive growth, with revenue rising from about $390 million in 2020 to more than $2.5 billion in 2022.

93. In Australia, selling or renting X-rated pornographic material is illegal in every state except the Australian Capital Territory and the Northern Territory, where it's permitted under strict regulation. Elsewhere, X-rated content can be legally owned but not commercially distributed.

94. Repeated exposure to sexual stimuli can lead to desensitization, pushing some users toward more frequent or more extreme content to achieve the same effect. Over time, that escalation can shift what someone finds arousing in ways they didn't anticipate. A small minority may slide from aggressive mainstream themes toward illegal material, which is a serious public-safety concern.

95. On professional sets, it's acting first. Near-strangers can switch from small talk to intense acts at "action," then stop mid-motion the instant "cut" is called. The intimacy is choreographed to the camera, not chemistry.

96. Some glamour modeling platforms serve as informal pipelines into the adult industry. When mainstream opportunities fall through, recruiters may subtly shift the pitch toward adult work, blurring the line between suggestive and explicit content. The transition from "cheesecake" modeling to hardcore material can be gradual and coercively framed as a fallback or next step.

97. In a survey from Men's Health and Women's Health, 72% of people surveyed said they would be open to tuning in to porn with their partner if he or she requested it.

98. In his socially radical pornographic work *Justine*, published in 1791, the Marquis de Sade details orgiastic scenes with long philosophical debates on the evils of property and traditional social hierarchy.

99. The online pornography industry is massive, generating over $3,000 every second while drawing nearly 30 million unique viewers in the same span of time. Pornographic material makes up a huge share of online activity, with 2.5 billion pornographic emails sent daily — about 8% of all emails — and more than 35% of all Internet downloads being adult content. Moreover, each day, pornography accounts for about 25% of all Internet searches.

100. A 2024 study found that couples who watch porn together often report feeling closer and more sexually satisfied, especially when both partners are on the same page about it. Where things can wobble is mismatched solo use—if one partner uses it a lot and the other rarely does, satisfaction tends to dip—and big-picture reviews still see a small overall negative link, stronger for women, so alignment and communication make the difference.

101. Porn has used almost every communication medium, including lithographs, the printing press, the Internet, photography, VHS, DVD, satellite TV, and more.

102. According to Pornhub, one of the world's largest adult sites, Americans spend the longest time per visit watching porn, averaging 10 minutes and 39 seconds per session. The U.K. ranked second, and Germany placed third in average viewing duration.

103. Research consistently shows that men respond sexually in a category-specific way — straight men become aroused predominantly by women, and gay men by men — while many women exhibit a category-nonspecific arousal pattern. Physiological studies, using methods like thermography and plethysmography, reveal that heterosexual women tend to show similar arousal to both male and female erotic stimuli, even if their self-reported preference is for one gender.

104. The advent of home video and the Internet has seen a boom in the porn industry worldwide.

105. By the 2020s, advances in artificial intelligence made it possible to create "deepfake pornography" — realistic synthetic videos that placed a person's face onto another body without consent. The technology spread rapidly across social media and adult sites, often targeting women and public figures. In response, governments in the U.S., U.K., and European Union began drafting and passing laws to criminalize the creation and distribution of non-consensual AI-generated sexual content, marking one of the first major global efforts to regulate artificial intelligence for ethical and privacy reasons.

106. The term "MILF," short for "Mom I'd Like to...," first gained mainstream recognition after the 1999 comedy *American Pie*, where it was used jokingly by teenage characters. It quickly became one of the most-searched adult keywords in the world.

107. The AVN Awards, often called "the Oscars of porn," have been held in Las Vegas every year since 1984 and celebrate categories ranging from cinematography to sound design — mirroring mainstream film structure.

108. When virtual-reality porn debuted commercially in 2016, it was the adult industry that pioneered most of the early VR camera rigs, viewer interfaces, and streaming methods now used in mainstream tech demos.

109. Ron Jeremy, once known as "The Hedgehog," became one of the most recognizable faces in adult film history, starring in more than 2,000 movies across four decades — more than any mainstream actor in Hollywood. Before his adult career, he earned a master's degree in special education and worked as a teacher. His unusual combination of academic background and unconventional looks helped him stand out in an industry dominated by stereotypes. However, his legacy later became overshadowed by over 30 sexual assault charges spanning decades, leading to his 2023 declaration as mentally unfit for trial. Once a symbol of the "Golden Age of Porn," Ron Jeremy's story has since become a cautionary tale about fame, abuse of power, and the darker sides of adult stardom.

110. Japan's adult industry is unique in that its censorship laws require pixelation of genitals, leading to a subculture of artistic workarounds that emphasize sound, expression, and context rather than explicit detail.

111. In 2022, the adult site Pornhub deleted millions of unverified videos in a single day after an investigation by *The New York Times* revealed illegal and non-consensual content on the platform.

112. The "Top 0.01%" badge on OnlyFans marks creators earning between $200,000 and over $1 million per month, serving as both a status symbol and proof of success. Creators on OnlyFans earn through subscriptions, tips, custom requests, and pay-per-view messages, with top earners diversifying into live streams, merchandise, and branding strategies.

3. Savage Nature & Shocking Wildlife

Nature doesn't do cute — it does brutal, bizarre, and utterly unhinged. From sex-changing animals to predators that devour their mates, the wild is full of shocking strategies for survival.

113. Pandas, often seen as cute and cuddly, are opportunistic carnivores that will eat fresh carcasses if found, revealing their surprisingly savage side.

114. Dogs are drawn to squeaky toys because the sound mimics the screams of prey. Many theories suggest they remove the squeaker because they perceive it as still alive, highlighting a primitive hunting instinct in domestic animals.

115. For male black widow spiders, mating is a deadly gamble. To succeed, the male must carefully position himself at a precise angle between the female's fangs, threading his way into danger just to transfer his sperm. Any mistake can mean instant death before reproduction even begins.

Even when the act is successful, the ordeal often ends the same way: the female turns on her partner and devours him, living up to her notorious name. Scientists believe this grim ritual may actually give the male an evolutionary advantage, since being eaten provides the female with nutrients that boost the survival chances of his offspring.

What seems like a gruesome betrayal is, in nature, a calculated trade — life for legacy, where mating and mortality are entwined in the same embrace.

116. A mosquito doesn't poke — it saws. Six needle-like stylets slice the skin, pry the wound, and deliver saliva loaded with anti-clotting, vasodilating compounds before the labrum draws blood. It's microsurgery with a built-in anticoagulant.

117. Botanically, berries must develop from a single ovary and have a specific layered structure with multiple seeds. Thus, bananas, eggplants,

and watermelons qualify as berries, while strawberries, raspberries, and blackberries are aggregate fruits despite their enduring, misleading common names.

118. Bloodworms harden their jaws with atacamite, a mineral form of copper, which not only sharpens their bite but also helps deliver venom more effectively. It's one of the rare times evolution turned heavy metal into a hunting tool.

119. Pandas have hidden sensual talents. Despite broad territories, male and female pandas are experts at locating one another just in time for ovulation. They do this by inspecting urine markings on trees that contain low-key chemical DTF messages. Moreover, fertile females often mate with several males to increase their chances of producing offspring.

120. Beetles are biodiversity's heavyweight champions. With roughly 400,000 described species — about a quarter of all known animal species — they fill nearly every niche on land. If evolution had a favorite design, it might be the elytra: the hardened forewings that protect and define beetles.

121. Some giant viruses, like mimivirus and pandoravirus, are so large and complex that they blur the line between virus and microbe. They can exceed many bacteria in both physical size and genome content. They challenge what we thought we knew about the simplicity of viruses.

122. Turritopsis dohrnii is the jellyfish that hits "retry." Under stress, the adult medusa can revert to a juvenile polyp and regrow, potentially looping the life cycle again and again. It's less a fountain of youth than a restart button.

123. Smaller marine iguanas apply auto-eroticism by rubbing themselves against rocks while advancing toward procreative females, which results in shorter lovemaking. Hence, bigger rivals are less likely to interrupt the smaller ones. Instead, it even increases their success in mating.

124. Mimosa pudica plants can remember being dropped and stop reacting to it, indicating possible plant memory and learning.

125. Lake Tanganyika's great age and isolation have turned it into a center of evolutionary diversity. It hosts hundreds of species that exist

nowhere else on Earth, including vividly colored cichlid fish and rare crustaceans. Its ancient, deep waters have nurtured a remarkable level of endemism found in few other places.

126. Monogamy is relatively rare in the animal kingdom, as strict fidelity can limit reproductive success. However, species that produce vulnerable offspring often remain loyal to a single mate. Birds are a prime example: because chicks need care from both parents, many bird species form monogamous pairs to ensure their young survive.

127. Sea cucumbers shoot their intestines as a defense mechanism.

128. Brown-headed cowbirds are notorious brood parasites, outsourcing the work of raising their chicks to other bird species. A female cowbird lays her eggs in a host's nest, leaving the unsuspecting parents to raise a chick that isn't their own. But if the hosts reject or destroy the cowbird egg, the adult cowbird may return to "punish" them — smashing eggs or wrecking the nest entirely before laying another. Scientists have dubbed this ruthless strategy the "mafia tactic."

129. That "fresh-cut grass" smell is chemistry for "I'm under attack." Plants release green leaf volatiles that warn neighboring leaves and summon predators of the herbivores doing the damage. Your summer nostalgia is a botanical distress call.

130. Most of Earth's volcanoes don't tower; they whisper underwater. Roughly three-quarters of volcanism happens along mid-ocean ridges where magma oozes out, cools, and builds new seafloor inch by inch. The planet remakes its skin in the dark.

131. Butterflies taste with their feet. Females drum leaves with sensory hairs to check the chemistry before laying eggs, and they test nectar the same way. It's daycare scouting done by footsteps.

132. Koalas possess fingerprints indistinguishable from humans under normal forensic methods. Their primate-like ridge pattern, unique among non-primates, theoretically could confuse crime-scene analysis — though koalas rarely frequent human burglary venues to muddy investigations with marsupial prints.

133. Echidnas have a 4-headed penis, which only emerges during erections and isn't used for urination.

134. Fleas store elastic energy and launch in about a millisecond, reaching roughly 100 g's of acceleration. Space shuttles peaked near 5 g's. Such forces would injure humans, but fleas' tiny bodies tolerate the extreme, instantaneous accelerative loads.

135. Antarctica is a frozen bank holding roughly 60 to 70% of Earth's fresh water. If it fully melted, global seas would rise on the order of 200 feet (about 60 meters). Whole coastlines would redraw overnight — geologically speaking.

136. Fungi are our distant cousins, not plant neighbors. They eat rather than photosynthesize, bank energy as glycogen, and build their walls from chitin — the same stuff in insect shells. Under a microscope, the family resemblance shows.

137. Cheetahs went through a severe population bottleneck thousands of years ago, leaving them highly inbred, making them unusually tolerant of skin grafts — but vulnerable to disease, infertility, and extinction. Genetic uniformity comes with a price.

138. The Amazon launches "flying rivers" — huge plumes of water vapor carried by winds across South America. Trees pump moisture skyward, and the atmosphere pipes it hundreds of miles to fall as rain elsewhere. It's a rainforest acting like a continent-scale sprinkler.

139. Antarctica's "Blood Falls" isn't gore — it's iron-rich brine seeping from a buried, salty reservoir. When the water hits air, the iron oxidizes and turns a shocking red. It's a rust fountain bleeding from ice.

140. A bite from the lone star tick can rewire your dinner menu. It can trigger alpha-gal syndrome, a delayed allergy to mammalian meat and products — hours after a burger, you break out or worse. One tick, and red meat becomes Russian roulette.

141. A narwhal's tusk is actually an elongated upper canine tooth, spiraling straight through its face. In rare cases, both canines erupt, giving the animal 2 unicorn-like tusks. What looks magical is really just extreme dentistry.

142. Pistol shrimp snap their claws fast enough to create cavitation bubbles in water. When those bubbles collapse, they generate a burst of heat near 8,540 degrees Fahrenheit (4,727 degrees Celsius) — briefly hotter than the sun's surface. The shockwave is strong enough to stun or kill nearby prey.

143. During metamorphosis, a caterpillar's body essentially dissolves. Most tissues break down into a cellular "soup," while tough little clusters called imaginal discs survive intact and rebuild the butterfly from scratch. Transformation, in this case, is total.

144. The WO virus, which infects parasitic Wolbachia bacteria, carries an eerie genetic signature: it has incorporated genes from black widow spiders, including those that code for venom. Scientists believe this unusual genetic borrowing may help the virus manipulate or evade the immune systems of its hosts, giving it a sinister advantage.

This kind of cross-species gene transfer is extremely rare, making the WO virus a striking example of nature's genetic creativity — or brutality. By blending viral, bacterial, and spider DNA, it blurs the boundaries between species and showcases how evolution can weaponize genetic material in unexpected ways. Researchers are only beginning to understand its implications, but the WO virus stands as a chilling reminder that viruses aren't just pathogens; they are genetic thieves, capable of rewriting life's code in ways both fascinating and frightening.

145. Due to artificial selection, dogs are evolving to have expressive eyebrows, demonstrating human influence on animal physiology in subtle but unsettling ways.

146. Squashing ants doesn't stop an infestation — surviving ants collect the crushed bodies and recycle them as food. Since only about 5% of a colony is outside the nest at any time, the rest of the ants continue their work undisturbed, efficiently scavenging every resource they can find.

147. The East African Rift is unzipping a continent in slow motion. Volcanoes, faults, and widening valleys mark the line where Africa will eventually split — leaving a newborn ocean basin in a few million years. Today it's farmland and roads; tomorrow (geologically speaking) it's seafloor.

148. The cleaner wrasse, a small reef fish, passed the mirror "mark test" often used to assess self-awareness. It tried to remove a visible mark on its body after seeing its reflection. The finding hints at unexpected intelligence beneath the waves.

149. Cuttlefish are masters of disguise and deception. They flash complex, rippling color patterns to blend into their surroundings or send signals to others. Some sneaky males even mimic females to slip past rivals and steal matings.

150. Everest's summit holds seashells in stone. The limestones up top are packed with marine fossils — remnants of the Tethys seafloor that got crumpled skyward when India slammed into Asia.

151. Crows are among the most intelligent creatures in the animal kingdom, with abilities that rival those of primates. Studies have shown they can recognize and remember human faces, distinguishing between people who treated them kindly and those who posed a threat. Once a crow decides someone is dangerous, it won't just hold a grudge — it will warn others.

These warnings aren't limited to a single flock. Crows are capable of passing this knowledge to their offspring, creating a kind of generational memory network. Decades later, a crow that has never encountered a particular person may still react defensively because its parents or community taught it to do so.

Beyond facial recognition, crows have demonstrated tool use, problem-solving, and even the ability to plan for the future — abilities once thought to be uniquely human. They aren't just birds watching from telephone wires; they're keen observers building mental maps of the world around them, remembering kindness and cruelty alike.

152. Sloths don't need muscles to hang from trees — their flexor tendons lock automatically when relaxed. It's so efficient that they can stay clinging even after death. Nature built them to hang on, literally.

153. Male alligators don't erect penises their whole lives. National Geographic demonstrated how their genitals spurt out like toothpaste from its tube. It then bounces back as if it's attached to a rubber band.

154. Italy's Stromboli volcano has been erupting steadily for thousands of years. Its frequent small blasts light up the night, earning it the nickname "The Lighthouse of the Mediterranean." Sailors have used its glow for navigation since ancient times.

155. Freshly cut grass releases green leaf volatiles — chemical distress signals warning neighboring plants of damage. The scent can attract predators of herbivorous insects, amplifying community defenses, even though plants can't escape lawnmowers and other large mechanical threats.

156. Convergent evolution has led to the independent emergence of crab-like forms in crustaceans at least 5 separate times — a phenomenon known as "carcinization." Despite not all being closely related to true crabs, different lineages evolved a similar compact, armored, sideways-scuttling body shape, likely due to shared environmental pressures favoring that efficient design.

157. The Namib is a desert with seniority, likely 55-plus million years old. Fog creeps in from the cold Atlantic while rain mostly stays away, preserving dunes older than entire mountain ranges. It's a museum of dryness still open for visitors.

158. Earth is awash in viruses — on the order of 10^{31} particles, mostly bacteriophages that prey on microbes. They pop cells, shuffle genes, and help drive nutrient cycles in oceans and soils. There are more of them than stars in the observable universe.

159. "Marine snow" is the ocean's slow, dark blizzard — flakes of dead plankton, poop pellets, and tiny carcasses drifting to the abyss. Down there, it feeds hungry communities and locks carbon away for centuries or millennia.

160. Blobfish only look "melted" when hauled to the surface. Built for crushing deep-sea pressure, they slump into that famous frown when decompressed; in their native depths, they're firmer, tadpole-shaped fish.

161. Many animals navigate using Earth's magnetic field. Proposed mechanisms include iron deposits functioning as tiny compasses, electromag-

netic induction in aquatic species, and cryptochrome proteins in eyes — possibly involving quantum effects — guiding migratory birds and sea turtles across vast distances with startling accuracy.

162. Pets can be allergic to humans. Our dander can act as an allergen, just like pet dander bothers us. Though uncommon — perhaps around 2 percent — human-allergic dogs or cats may show itching, sneezing, or skin irritation triggered by their owners.

163. There are an estimated 20 quadrillion ants on Earth — about 2.5 million for every person. While older claims suggested their total biomass rivaled that of humans, newer research shows humans now outweigh them. With around 71% of ant species possessing venom, a hypothetical human-versus-ants showdown would likely not end in our favor.

164. Cockroaches have been documented consuming human flesh, fingernails, eyelashes, feet, and hands, both from living and deceased humans. The American cockroach and German cockroach are particularly likely to bite humans, making them disturbing survivors in human habitats.

165. A newly discovered Costa Rican fly species has males with genital spines longer than their bodies, used in mating and combat.

166. Oysters have organs like a stomach, heart, and muscles, and while they lack a brain, they may still react to harm through their nervous system.

167. Venus flytraps don't just react — they count. Two touches from a prey item snap the trap shut, but around 5 more are needed to trigger digestion, likely through accumulating electrical signals.

168. Animals that are less stressed before slaughter produce fresher meat due to higher glycogen levels converting to lactic acid postmortem.

169. Sinkholes are geology's trapdoors, usually forming where water dissolves bedrock like limestone or gypsum and leaves hidden voids — classic karst terrain. Pave a road or build over those cavities, add heavy rain, leaking pipes, over-pumped groundwater, or nearby mining, and a "cover-collapse" can happen fast: street one minute, crater the next.

170. The sea slug Elysia chlorotica steals chloroplasts from algae and keeps them running inside its own cells. With those hijacked "solar panels," it can photosynthesize for months, blurring the line between animal and leaf. It's kleptomania as a survival strategy.

4. Crazy Creations & Accidental Inventions

Human creativity is messy, brilliant, and sometimes catastrophic. Serendipitous discoveries, bizarre experiments, and deadly innovations reveal just how strange progress can be.

171. In 1945, Percy Spencer noticed that a chocolate bar had melted in his pocket while he was working near radar equipment. This unexpected discovery led to experiments with food and ultimately to the invention of the microwave oven — a breakthrough that transformed cooking forever.

172. Alexander Bogdanov believed blood transfusions were the key to immortality. After self-administering 11 transfusions, he took a final one from a donor infected with malaria and tuberculosis. The infusion proved fatal.

173. Britain's Cold War plan to bury nuclear landmines in Germany ran into a problem: electronics might freeze in winter. The proposed solution was to keep chickens inside the bomb casings for warmth. Thankfully, this bizarre idea never moved beyond the planning stage.

174. In the early 1800s, John Walker accidentally invented matches when a chemically coated stick caught fire as he scraped it. He refused to patent the idea, believing it should help humanity freely. His matches became popular worldwide.

175. Thomas Edison built a prolific "invention factory" at Menlo Park, where teams of researchers developed new technologies that were typically patented under Edison's name. The collaborative model helped pioneer modern corporate R&D, streamlining innovation at scale. However, it also complicated the legacy of individual credit, blurring the line between Edison's personal contributions and those of his team.

176. Those groovy polyester suits from the disco era were cheap, wrinkle-resistant, and dangerously flammable. Unlike cotton or wool, polyester would melt into human skin when ignited, causing third-degree burns. It took a wave of horrifying injuries before fire-safety standards caught up.

177. In 1945, scientists racing under the Manhattan Project split the atom and changed the world. The first combat use came within days: on August 6, a single bomb turned Hiroshima's morning sky white; on August 9, Nagasaki followed. Tens of thousands died in seconds, and many more in the weeks that followed. The survivors — later called hibakusha — carried burns, cancers, and grief for the rest of their lives, living proof that radiation's damage lingers long after the blast fades.

Japan surrendered soon after, and for some, the bombs seemed to have ended the war that nothing else could. But the victory arrived with a terrible price: the knowledge that human hands could erase a city in an instant. The U.S.' monopoly didn't last. The Soviet Union tested its own bomb in 1949, and the Cold War hardened into a standoff built on arsenals and doctrines — deterrence, brinkmanship, and mutually assured destruction. Sirens, drills, and shelter plans became part of ordinary life.

Decades later, the debate endures. Did the bombs shorten the war and save lives that would have been lost in an invasion, or did they inaugurate an age of fear and mass death that might have been avoided? What is certain is their legacy: a pair of detonations that ended one catastrophe by unleashing a new one — the permanent shadow of nuclear possibility over human history.

178. Fireworks in the 1970s were loaded with toxic metals like lead and copper to create brilliant colors. But the dazzling displays released poisonous particles into the air and soil. These heavy metals damaged lungs, tainted ecosystems, and harmed wildlife — all for a few minutes of entertainment.

179. In 1984, Carol "Nathan Boya" Suits made headlines by surviving a 180-foot (55-meter) drop over Niagara Falls inside a barrel of his own design. Seeking to push the limits further, he attempted a stunt at the Houston Astrodome with a new shock-absorbing barrel. But when the barrel missed its intended water tank, the impact proved fatal, turning his pursuit of spectacle into tragedy.

180. Isaac Singer built a sewing machine empire using a mechanism that closely resembled one patented by Elias Howe. When Howe sued for patent infringement, the legal battle was intense — but he ultimately

prevailed. The court awarded him royalties from Singer's sales, securing both financial compensation and lasting credit for his pivotal invention.

181. Alfred Nobel invented dynamite in 1867 as a more stable and manageable form of nitroglycerin, revolutionizing construction and mining. However, its rapid adoption for warfare and acts of political violence deeply troubled him. Haunted by the destructive legacy of his invention, Nobel sought to redefine how he would be remembered — leading him to establish the Nobel Prizes as a lasting contribution to peace, science, and humanity.

182. Sylvester Roper's steam-powered velocipede — an early ancestor of the motorcycle — never reached mass production, but it did carry him to his grave. In 1896, during a test ride, Roper suffered a heart attack, lost control, and crashed, making him one of the earliest casualties of motorized transport.

183. French chemist Édouard Bénédictus accidentally dropped a glass beaker coated with plastic residue and was surprised when it cracked but didn't shatter. Inspired by the accident, he developed safety glass, which became widely used in car windshields and protective gear. His discovery has saved countless lives by preventing deadly shards in accidents.

184. Early friction matches relied on white phosphorus, a toxic substance that posed serious health risks to factory workers. Prolonged exposure to its fumes caused "phossy jaw," a horrifying condition in which the jawbone decayed and sometimes emitted a faint glow in the dark. It wasn't until the early 20th century that safer red phosphorus formulations began to replace it, dramatically reducing these dangers.

185. Michael Dacre dreamed of transforming city travel with the Jetpod, a compact, low-noise aircraft designed to land in tight urban spaces. But in 2009, during a solo test flight in Malaysia, the prototype stalled and crashed just seconds after takeoff, killing him instantly. His ambitious vision for airborne taxis ended before it could take flight.

186. During World War 2, actress Hedy Lamarr and composer George Antheil invented a spread-spectrum radio system intended to prevent enemy jamming of torpedo signals. Though the U.S. Navy initially shelved the idea, it later incorporated the technology quietly. Decades

later, Lamarr finally received public recognition, as their concept became a cornerstone of modern wireless communication technologies like Wi-Fi and Bluetooth.

187. The British built a rocket-powered wheel called the Great Panjandrum to breach Nazi defenses. During public tests, it spun out of control, crashed unpredictably, and even endangered top military officials. After repeated failures and near disasters, the project was scrapped in embarrassment.

188. Thomas Edison's kinetoscope, one of the earliest film-viewing machines, was celebrated as a technological breakthrough. However, its most profitable early use wasn't for wholesome storytelling — it was for erotic "peep shows" viewed individually in back rooms. In fact, some of the first major profits in cinema came not from high art, but from risqué content that catered to curiosity and taboo.

189. Alexander Graham Bell's telephone success overshadowed Antonio Meucci, who had demonstrated a similar device earlier. Meucci's prototype conveniently went "missing," and only recently has his priority gained wider historical support.

190. John North developed a vacuum system and shared it with Electrolux under a nondisclosure agreement. Despite this, the company went on to manufacture and sell millions of units based on his design without permission.

191. John Day, a carpenter-turned-inventor, built one of the earliest experimental submarines in 1774 and wagered he could survive underwater for 12 hours. But his wooden craft was poorly designed, and during its trial run it sank rapidly. Day never resurfaced, making him one of history's first submarine casualties.

192. In 1718, the Puckle gun — an early attempt at a machine gun — came with a strange twist. Its inventor suggested firing round bullets at Christians and square ones at everyone else, supposedly to scare them more. It was part weapon, part propaganda, and all bizarre. The gun never took off, but its warped ideology still leaves a chill.

193. In 1903, William Nelson, a General Electric employee, unveiled his invention — a motorized bicycle. But on its very first test ride, the machine malfunctioned and hurled him to the ground, killing him instantly. The design never advanced beyond that ill-fated debut.

194. In 1989, a U.S. submarine's test launch of a Trident II missile went catastrophically wrong. Instead of soaring skyward, the missile spun wildly in circles just above the water before crashing back into the sea, narrowly missing the vessel itself. Investigators later discovered the rocket nozzle had been blocked by water, causing the dramatic failure.

195. PCBs, once praised as fireproof "miracle chemicals," were widely used in insulation, transformers, and electrical equipment. But over time, they accumulated in people and wildlife, causing cancer, immune system dysfunction, and reproductive harm. Even after their U.S. ban in 1979, old devices continued leaking toxins into soil and rivers, and the compounds hardly break down. Decades later, PCBs still linger in buildings, landfills, and ecosystems, with cleanup efforts proving costly, hazardous, and far from complete.

196. Candy cigarettes once let children mimic smoking, even producing sugary "puffs" of fake smoke. But research later showed that kids who played with them were more likely to start smoking for real. Because of their role in glamorizing addiction, they've been banned or heavily restricted in many countries.

197. Even ordinary household gadgets and drinks in the 1970s, from building materials to soda cans, were ticking time bombs. Many were poorly tested, lightly regulated, and sold before their true dangers were understood. It was a decade of bold innovation — and sometimes lethal consequences.

198. In the late 19th and early 20th centuries, vibrating belt machines were marketed as cutting-edge weight-loss devices. Users would strap in and be vigorously shaken, supposedly to "jiggle away" fat. Despite lacking scientific support — and causing injuries such as spinal strain and internal damage — the machines became popular fixtures in health clubs, touted as modern, science-backed fitness technology.

199. Leo Baekeland created plastic while trying to replace expensive shellac made from beetles. His new material was moldable and heat-resistant. It became the foundation of the plastic age.

200. Rockets were originally Chinese inventions, but modern rocketry was shaped by Wernher von Braun, whose V-2 missiles killed over 7,000 people during World War 2. Production of these weapons also cost the lives of 12,000 forced laborers.

201. In 1968, Spencer Silver invented a weak adhesive by accident while trying to make a strong one. It was later used for Post-it Notes after a colleague needed bookmarks. The product became a global office staple.

202. DDT was once celebrated as a miracle pesticide, praised for controlling malaria-carrying mosquitoes and boosting crop yields. But its dark legacy soon emerged: it accumulated in soil and water, weakened bird eggshells, and nearly wiped out species like the bald eagle. Rachel Carson's Silent Spring exposed its dangers, leading to a U.S. ban in 1972. Today, DDT is remembered as both a lifesaver and a poisoner of entire ecosystems.

203. In the 1970s, engineers experimented with powering pacemakers using plutonium-238, hoping to create devices that would last a lifetime without battery changes. The idea carried chilling risks: if the casing cracked during surgery or an accident, radioactive material could leak into the patient's body. Disposal posed another problem, since the tiny reactors inside couldn't simply be discarded as medical waste, making the nuclear pacemaker an invention too dangerous to continue.

204. Nazi engineers attempted to develop a curved-barrel rifle, known as the Krummlauf, to allow soldiers to shoot around corners. However, the design warped bullets, wore out rapidly, and often shattered projectiles inside the barrel. Though briefly deployed, it was quickly abandoned due to its impracticality.

205. Agent Orange, originally developed as an agricultural herbicide, was repurposed by the U.S. military during the Vietnam War to strip away forest cover. Laced with toxic dioxins, it poisoned landscapes and people alike, causing cancers, birth defects, and long-term environmental damage. Estimates link it to at least 400,000 deaths and disabilities and

over 500,000 birth defects. Decades later, both veterans and civilians continue to suffer its devastating legacy.

206. Mercury thermometers were standard in every household and school until we learned how toxic they were. A single broken thermometer could fill a room with vapor that damaged brains and kidneys. Eventually, governments phased them out for safer digital models.

207. Charles Annan tried to patent a flat-bottom paper bag machine that was actually Margaret E. Knight's creation. Her meticulous notebooks convinced the court to restore the patent to its rightful inventor.

208. Fiberglass insulation was marketed as a miracle in the '70s — lightweight, energy-efficient, and cheap. But early versions were so flammable they helped fires spread, not stop. Burning fiberglass also released toxic, cancer-causing fumes that made any house fire even more deadly.

209. Zyklon B, originally a pesticide invented in Germany, was used by the Nazis in gas chambers during the Holocaust. Roughly one million people were killed with it at Auschwitz and other extermination camps.

210. Shoe stores in the 1950s and 60s had unshielded X-ray machines that kids would use to see their foot bones inside new shoes. They were still around in some places in the '70s before finally getting banned. Repeated exposure led to radiation burns, cancer, and genetic damage in both customers and store clerks.

211. In World War 2, Japan launched nearly 9,000 incendiary balloons aimed at the U.S., hoping they'd start massive wildfires. Most failed and landed in the Pacific, but one balloon in Oregon killed a pregnant woman and 5 children. It was the only fatal incident, yet the attack was kept secret to avoid encouraging further strikes.

212. The brazen bull, an ancient Greek execution device designed to roast victims alive inside a bronze chamber shaped like a bull, carried a grim twist of fate. Its inventor, Perillos of Athens, proposed it to Phalaris, the tyrant of Acragas — who, according to legend, ordered Perillos to be the first to die in it, executed in the very creation he had designed.

213. Max Valier strapped rockets to sleds and cars in the 1920s to excite public interest in space travel. His pursuit of liquid-fueled rocketry ended

in tragedy when an experimental engine exploded, fatally piercing his lung with shrapnel.

214. Though now associated with forestry — or horror films — the chainsaw was originally invented in the late 18th century by 2 Scottish surgeons as a medical device. Its original purpose was to cut through bone and cartilage during difficult childbirth procedures, such as symphysiotomies.

215. Charles Darrow is often credited with creating Monopoly, but the game's original concept was developed by Elizabeth Magie decades earlier. Her version, The Landlord's Game, was designed to critique economic inequality and monopolies. While Darrow's adaptation became a commercial success, Magie's contribution went largely unrecognized until long after her death.

216. Valerian Abakovsky's "Aerowagon" combined rail travel with aircraft propulsion. During a return trip from a test run in 1921, the vehicle derailed at high speed, killing everyone on board — including its inventor.

217. Early aluminum soda and beer cans exploded randomly on store shelves due to weak construction and internal pressure miscalculations. People suffered cuts, eye injuries, and even permanent damage just trying to grab a drink. Beverage companies had to redesign the entire can industry from the inside out.

218. The AK-47, invented by Russian engineer Mikhail Kalashnikov, became a symbol of military power for its reliability. It also fueled countless conflicts and mass casualties across the globe. Kalashnikov himself later expressed regret over its use in violence.

219. Roy J. Plunkett discovered Teflon in the 1930s while working on safer refrigerator gases. A strange residue he found turned out to be nonstick, heat-resistant, and chemically stable. It became a DuPont patent and a modern kitchen essential.

220. When inventor Robert Kearns pitched his design for the intermittent windshield wiper, both Ford and Chrysler turned him down — only to later implement nearly identical systems in their vehicles. Kearns took them to court, representing himself for much of the legal battle. He ulti-

mately won millions in settlements and was legally recognized as the rightful inventor.

221. In 1957, doctors noticed that the tuberculosis drug iproniazid elevated patients' moods, transforming a failed tuberculosis treatment into the first antidepressant and opening a new era in psychiatry.

222. Carl Wilhelm Scheele was an 18th-century chemist who discovered oxygen and several other elements. Unfortunately, his dangerous habit of tasting the chemicals he worked with likely contributed to his death from mercury poisoning.

223. Wilson Greatbatch accidentally installed the wrong resistor while building a heart monitor, and the device began emitting steady electrical pulses. Realizing the potential, he refined the design into the first implantable pacemaker. By 1960, it was successfully used in patients, revolutionizing cardiac care.

5. Weird Science & Cosmic Oddities

Science stretches from the microscopic to the cosmic. Stem cells mimic life, electrons split into pieces, black holes can form from pure light, and the universe is mostly empty — a reminder that reality is stranger than fiction.

224. Scientists can reprogram adult cells into induced pluripotent stem cells, genetically matched to the donor. These cells can become any tissue type, enabling research on patient-specific therapies, organ-on-chip models, and future prospects for lab-grown, rejection-resistant organs.

225. In 2012, 10-year-old Clara Lazen built a novel molecular model in class. Chemists realized it represented a feasible compound, tetranitratoxycarbon. Simulations suggested interesting energy-storage or explosive properties; Lazen and her teacher were credited on the paper.

226. In theoretical physics, a black hole could form purely from concentrated radiation — a concept known as a kugelblitz. Because energy, like mass, can bend spacetime, an extremely dense burst of light could create an event horizon. It's a black hole formed not from matter, but from energy alone.

227. The Casimir effect is the vacuum's quiet handshake. Put 2 uncharged metal plates absurdly close together, and the altered quantum fluctuations between them nudge the plates inward. It's a force from "nothing," measured in labs with patience and polish.

228. In some exotic materials, an electron seems to split its identity. Its charge, spin, and orbital motion peel off into separate quasiparticles — holons, spinons, and orbitons — that move independently through the lattice.

229. Strange matter, a hypothetical form of ultra-stable quark matter, could convert all normal matter into strangelets upon contact, potentially destroying Earth or the universe. Though theoretical, high-energy collisions or cosmic events could trigger this runaway reaction.

230. On Mars, sunsets go blue. Fine dust and the thin carbon dioxide atmosphere scatter red light away, while forward-scattering lets more blue slip through right around the Sun. The sky reddens; the rim of daylight turns sapphire.

231. Tibetans carry genetic adaptations like EPAS1 that help them thrive at high altitudes. These changes allow for more efficient oxygen use, larger lung capacity, and lower hemoglobin levels. Evolution carved survival into their DNA — one breath at a time.

232. Despite holding billions of galaxies, each with billions of stars, space is almost entirely empty. The distances between celestial objects are so immense that a photon — or even a spacecraft — could travel for ages without hitting anything. Even when galaxies collide, their stars rarely crash into one another; instead, they slip silently past, separated by vast stretches of interstellar nothingness.

The emptiness makes space both terrifying and awe-inspiring. From Earth, the night sky looks crowded with light, yet what we see is a fraction of a universe where matter is rare, and true voids stretch for millions of light-years. Space is not a sea of stars but a near-perfect vacuum, a cosmic desert where gravity shapes islands of brilliance separated by incomprehensible gulfs. It's a reminder that everything familiar — planets, stars, life itself — exists as tiny sparks in an overwhelming darkness.

233. Surveys of botanical displays across dozens of museums found more than half of plant specimens mislabeled or incompletely labeled. Taxonomy shifts, limited experts, and difficult identifications contribute, highlighting how dynamic and challenging biological classification remains in practice.

234. Io is a volcanic powerhouse, sculpted by gravity. Jupiter's immense pull — amplified by orbital resonance with Europa and Ganymede — flexes Io's interior, generating heat and driving relentless eruptions.

235. Photons take about 8 and a half minutes to travel from the Sun to Earth, but energy takes 100,000+ years to random-walk from the core to the surface. Photons are repeatedly absorbed and re-emitted; the "burp" that emerges isn't the original particles.

236. Exoplanet Gliese 436b, a "hot Neptune," likely hosts superheated high-pressure ice that remains solid near approximately 980 degrees Fahrenheit (about 527 degrees Celsius). Pressure, not temperature, stabilizes the exotic ice phase — an extreme reminder that alien worlds defy Earth-based intuitions about water.

237. Thermoluminescence dating turns heat into a clock. Minerals trap electrical charge from background radiation; when a pot or brick last met the kiln, that clock was reset. Reheating the sample today makes it glow, and the glow counts the years since the last fire.

238. The "dark flow" is one of the most puzzling discoveries in modern cosmology. First identified in 2008, it describes an enormous movement of galaxy clusters — massive chunks of the universe's largest structures — all drifting in the same direction, as though being pulled by some unseen force. What makes it so mysterious is that this motion doesn't line up with the expansion of the universe or any known gravitational sources.

Scientists have theorized that the dark flow might point to something beyond the observable universe, perhaps vast structures or even other universes exerting a gravitational pull. Yet, despite years of study, its cause and destination remain unknown. Some researchers have even questioned whether the effect is real or a product of measurement limits, but no definitive explanation has emerged.

239. Venus rotates retrograde — opposite most planets — likely due to an ancient, massive impact. Uranus spins on its side, probably from a similar collision. Elsewhere in the cosmos, stellar and planetary spin directions vary widely, showing no universal preferred orientation.

240. Earth's day lengthens by about 1.7 milliseconds per century as lunar tides brake rotation. Hundreds of millions of years ago, days were shorter. Given eons, Earth and Moon could tidally lock — but the Sun's evolution will intervene first.

241. The Sahara wasn't always a sea of sand. During the African Humid Period, it was a green land dotted with lakes and rivers. Ancient rock art shows people herding cattle across grassy plains, and fossils confirm the wildlife that once thrived there. It's a reminder of how quickly climates can flip a landscape from fertile to forbidding.

242. Microplastics and nanoplastics — formed as plastic fragments — are now found in air, snow, oceans, lungs, blood, and intestines. Human health effects remain uncertain; animal studies raise concerns, but suitable human controls are scarce because microplastic exposure is nearly ubiquitous.

243. The brightest and hottest supernova ever recorded, ASASSN-15lh, reached an astonishing temperature of about 180 billion degrees Fahrenheit (100 billion degrees Celsius) and shone with a brightness roughly 570 billion times greater than our Sun.

244. Astronomers have detected giant interstellar clouds of alcohol, including methanol, near Sagittarius B, thousands of light-years away. Quantities are mind-boggling — far beyond human use — but it's toxic methanol, not drinkable ethanol, and offers clues to complex chemistry in star-forming regions.

245. Many scientists believe the universe won't end with a bang but with a slow, inevitable fading into nothingness — a scenario known as "heat death." Over trillions of years, galaxies will drift so far apart that their light will never reach one another. Stars will exhaust their fuel and wink out, leaving only cold remnants. Even black holes will evaporate, and the very atoms that make up matter will eventually decay.

In this distant future, energy will be perfectly balanced, with no gradients to power motion, light, or life. The cosmos will become a silent, eternal void, where time continues but nothing happens. Heat death is not an explosion or a collapse, but a quiet erasure — a reminder that the universe's greatest enemy is not chaos, but equilibrium, and that all creation may one day dissolve into an endless, frozen dark.

246. Helium was discovered in the Sun before it was found on Earth. In 1868, astronomers spotted a strange yellow spectral line during a solar eclipse and named a new element after Helios, the Sun. Only in 1895 did chemists finally isolate it down here.

247. St. Elmo's fire is a faint blue or violet glow that appears on pointed objects — like ship masts, church steeples, or airplane wings — during powerful electrical storms. It's created when plasma forms in the air due

to strong electric fields. For centuries, sailors viewed it with awe, interpreting it as either a warning or a protective sign from the heavens.

248. Researchers have discovered that certain genes related to brain activity can reactivate hours or even days after clinical death. The surprising phenomenon has led scientists to question traditional definitions of death and explore the possibility that some cellular functions may persist far longer than previously believed.

249. Astronomers have detected a quasar's host cloud holding over 100 trillion times the water in Earth's oceans, which dates back to the early universe, proving that water has been around for billions of years. The cosmos has been wet far longer than Earth has existed.

250. Mitochondria have their own DNA, inherited mostly from the mothers. They divide and function independently inside our cells, echoing their bacterial origins. An odd autonomy that supports the theory that mitochondria were once free-living organisms.

251. The Sun's long goodbye is scripted. It will swell into a red giant, puff off its outer layers into a glowing nebula, and retire as an Earth-sized white dwarf — a hot ember of carbon and oxygen cooling for eons. Same star, very different silhouette.

252. Pluto was named by 11-year-old Venetia Burney, a schoolgirl from England. She suggested the name to her grandfather, who happened to have connections in the astronomical community and passed it along. The astronomers approved, and her idea became official. A child's suggestion gave the solar system one of its most debated and distant members.

253. Israeli scientists created the world's first synthetic embryo from stem cells, complete with a brain, heart, and intestines — raising profound ethical questions.

254. In the late 1780s, a Swedish army lieutenant named Carl Axel Arrhenius picked up a heavy, sooty-black stone from a quarry in the village of Ytterby, just outside Stockholm. Chemists tore the sample apart for decades, teasing new "earths" out of its stubborn mix: first yttria (from which yttrium was named), then further splits that revealed terbium and erbium, and later ytterbium. What began as a single curious rock turned

into a naming cascade, putting the same tiny village on the periodic table 4 separate times.

Ytterby's quarry didn't just mint names; it jump-started an era of rare-earth chemistry that still underpins modern tech. The elements first isolated from their minerals now glow in smartphone screens, sharpen medical imaging, and tune lasers and fiber-optic lines. For a place barely large enough to notice on a map, Ytterby left fingerprints all over the elements — and, by extension, over the devices in our pockets.

255. Cosmic rays transform the upper atmosphere into a particle factory. Their collisions trigger showers that produce positrons, which quickly meet electrons and annihilate into gamma rays. Antimatter is constantly being created and destroyed above our heads.

256. Venus is uninhabitable due to its scorching surface temperature of about 932 degrees Fahrenheit (500 degrees Celsius), crushing atmospheric pressure that's roughly 90 times greater than Earth's, and relentless clouds of sulfuric acid rain. These extreme conditions make it one of the most hostile environments in the solar system.

257. A standard 52-card deck can be arranged in about 8.1×10^{67} different ways — more than the estimated number of atoms in the Milky Way. Every proper shuffle almost certainly produces a sequence that has never existed before, showcasing the staggering power of factorial growth.

258. There is no sound in space because sound needs particles to travel through. In the vacuum of space, it's completely silent — unless you're inside a dense gas cloud.

259. Around 2 billion years ago in Oklo, Gabon, natural uranium deposits achieved self-sustaining nuclear fission — without any help from humans. These ancient reactors ran intermittently for hundreds of thousands of years. It's the only known case of natural nuclear power on Earth.

260. Heat can erase magnetism the way noise drowns out a melody. Above a material's Curie temperature, thermal jostling scrambles magnetic domains and the magnet goes limp — only to snap back when it cools and order returns.

261. Bismuth is technically radioactive, but its decay is unimaginably slow — with a half-life of around 20 quintillion years. That's roughly a billion times the age of the universe, making it completely safe to handle.

262. In space, astronauts' calluses and dead skin begin to flake off after a month, especially from their feet, due to the lack of pressure and friction.

263. Vaccines can unintentionally fuel virus evolution. For example, *pertussis* (or whooping cough) resurged in some countries after the switch from whole-cell to acellular vaccines, partly because the bacteria adapted to escape immune responses. Similarly, the hepatitis B virus has shown mutations in its surface antigen that allow it to evade vaccine-induced immunity, raising concerns about "vaccine escape" strains.

264. Quasars, found at the centers of active galaxies, are the most powerful, luminous, and energetic objects in the universe — emitting over 1,000 times the energy of the Milky Way.

265. Some exoplanets may be tidally locked, always showing one face to their star. These so-called "eyeball planets" might have one liquid hemisphere — either scorched or icy — surrounded by a frozen ring. Alien worlds could be half ocean, half wasteland.

A teaspoon of neutron-star matter would weigh about 6 billion tons (about 5.4 metric tons) — roughly 1,000 Great Pyramids of Giza compressed into a spoonful. Neutron stars, collapsed stellar cores, pack nuclei-dense matter where electrons and protons merge into closely packed neutrons.

266. A theoretical concept called a white hole is the reverse of a black hole — nothing can enter, and everything escapes, including light. Some believe they may be linked to black holes.

267. Falling into a black hole could lead to a process known as "spaghettification," where the body is stretched and compressed by intense gravitational forces. Some theories also suggest that the extreme time distortion near a black hole's event horizon could create split realities or alternate timelines.

268. Underwater eruptions can form "pillow lava": rapid quenching by

seawater skins the lava while the interior keeps flowing, inflating rounded bulbs that record ancient oceans on Earth.

269. If the Sun exploded right now, Earth wouldn't notice for 8 minutes and 20 seconds — the time it takes light and energy to travel the 93 million miles (150 million kilometers) between the Sun and Earth.

270. PET scanners work using antimatter. They release positrons, which annihilate with electrons in the body, producing paired gamma rays. By tracing those rays, doctors can map metabolic activity in stunning detail.

271. Saturn's rings are geologically young and already fading. Micrometeoroids and Saturn's gravity are pulling the icy grains inward as "ring rain," dooming the spectacle in a few hundred million years.

272. Most of the world's coal formed during the Carboniferous period, over 300 million years ago. Back then, swampy forests buried plant material faster than microbes could break it down. Over time, pressure turned those ancient bogs into black rock.

273. Although alien life likely exists given the scale of the universe, we may never find it due to the accelerating expansion of the universe and limitations in space travel.

274. Cosmologists have long debated how the universe might end, and 2 of the most striking theories offer opposite fates. The Big Crunch proposes that the universe's expansion will eventually slow, halt, and reverse under the pull of gravity. Galaxies would begin to drift back together, stars would collide, and all matter would collapse into an unimaginably dense state — a catastrophic rewind of the Big Bang.

The Big Rip, by contrast, imagines a future where expansion never stops. Instead, it accelerates, stretching the fabric of space-time so rapidly that galaxies, stars, planets, and eventually even atoms themselves are torn apart. In this scenario, the universe ends not in a crushing implosion but in infinite fragmentation, unraveling reality piece by piece.

275. In about a trillion years, the night sky may go completely black, as stars move farther away and become invisible.

276. Most of the observable universe is unreachable in practice. Even traveling at light speed, expansion limits us to regions within roughly a 17-billion-light-year starting radius. About 86% of observable galaxies are forever inaccessible without exotic spacetime shortcuts.

277. Most of Earth's gold sank into the core when the planet differentiated. If you could haul it all back up and spread it evenly, you'd plate the world in roughly half a meter of the stuff. Our jewelry is just the crumbs that never fell.

278. Only about 5% of the universe is made up of matter we can observe; the remaining 95% consists of dark matter and dark energy, which remain mysterious and unmeasured.

279. A diamond is just carbon dressed up in its hardest form. Put it under enough heat in the presence of oxygen, and it doesn't shatter — it burns, turning into plain old carbon dioxide. Even the toughest gem on Earth bows to the oldest rule in chemistry: carbon plus fire makes smoke.

280. Some researchers have proposed that water has the ability to "remember" substances it has come into contact with — even after being diluted beyond the point where any molecules of the original material remain. This controversial idea, sometimes cited in homeopathy, suggests water retains a structural imprint of its history, carrying information in ways science cannot yet explain.

Mainstream research, however, has found no solid evidence to support this claim, and most scientists regard water memory as pseudoscience. Still, the concept persists, capturing public imagination and raising philosophical questions about how little we truly understand the world's most essential molecule.

281. Banana peels are remarkably slippery: their measured friction coefficient of about 0.07 is close to near-frictionless conditions underfoot. The polysaccharide gel inside the peel resembles joint synovial fluid, inspiring research that may one day improve artificial joint lubrication and reduce wear in biomedical implants.

282. "Dark oxygen" may form deep in sunless oceans through non-biological processes like radiolysis, where radiation splits water molecules. An

unexpected oxygen source that suggests life could endure in more places than once thought; even without sunlight, chemistry can keep oxygen-rich niches alive.

283. The Moon is gradually drifting away from Earth at a rate of about 1.6 inches (4 centimeters) per year. Over millions of years, this slow separation could impact ocean tides, sea levels, and even slightly alter the Earth's rotation.

6. Ghosts, Magic & Creepy Rituals

Strange lights, phantom footsteps, and spirits with unfinished business populate history and legend. Tales of ghostly brides, restless soldiers, and haunted homes show that the supernatural can be terrifying, mysterious, and oddly persistent.

284. In 18th-century England, Miss Beswick, terrified of being buried alive after her brother's near-entombment, wrote in her will that her body must never be buried. Her embalmed corpse was kept above ground for decades, even displayed in a museum, and ordered to be returned to her estate every 21 years. When she was finally buried, her ghost was soon reported gliding through her old home in a black dress, and strange lights and noises were heard from a barn said to conceal her treasure.

285. After being murdered by her husband in 1936, Doris Gravlin became known as the April Ghost, said to haunt Victoria Golf Course in British Columbia. Witnesses report seeing her appear each spring in a wedding dress, sometimes rushing at them before vanishing in a burst of light. Locals say her haunting is a grim warning to young couples about love and betrayal.

286. In the 1950s, plumber Harry Martindale claimed he saw a troop of Roman soldiers marching through the basement walls of the Treasurer's House in York. He described their green tunics, round shields, and distinctive gear in striking detail. Oddly, the soldiers appeared cut off at the knees — until later excavations revealed an ancient Roman road lying about 18 inches (46 centimeters) beneath the modern floor. Martindale kept quiet for 20 years, only sharing his story after others reported similar sightings.

287. In the late 1980s, Jackie Hernandez suffered a terrifying haunting in San Pedro, California. She reported disembodied voices, a floating ghostly head in her attic, and an incident where an invisible force nearly strangled a cameraman. Paranormal investigator Barry Taff linked the activity to a murdered sailor named Henderson. Even after moving away, Jackie claimed the spirit followed her.

288. Two officers in rural West Virginia responded to a late-night call about a strange creature near the roadside. The witness described a tall, pale figure with glowing eyes that vanished into the woods. As the officers investigated, they were overcome by an intense sense of dread and quickly retreated. When they returned later, the area was silent and empty — no creature, no tracks, nothing to explain what had happened.

289. In 2009, a student named Josh visited Gettysburg and encountered a Civil War ghost in the bathroom of the Hall of Presidents. While washing his hands, he saw a soldier with sideburns and a rifle standing beside him in the mirror. When he turned, the figure vanished, and a stall door opened by itself. A disembodied voice then screamed "Mine!" into his ear, terrifying him. A chaperone later told the group the museum was built over a mass grave.

290. Paranormal tour guide Carrie Willer worked at Nemacolin Castle and Brownsville Hospital in Pennsylvania, where she saw multiple full-body apparitions, including Civil War soldiers and Victorian women. One spirit wore yellow clogs that left footprints on a freshly waxed floor. In the old maternity ward, she and a coworker saw a ghost nurse return to the spot where cribs once stood. She also saw her deceased grandmother deliver a premonition that came true. Though unnerving, Carrie came to accept ghosts as a routine part of her work.

291. Anne Boleyn's ghost is said to haunt multiple historic sites in England, often appearing in white or carrying her severed head. Her most famous haunt is the Tower of London, but she has also been reported at Hever Castle, Blickling Hall, and Windsor. Some witnesses describe eerie headless horses and ghostly processions, forever tied to her execution.

292. In San Antonio, Texas, on the night of October 14, 2017, what began as a normal house party turned unsettling when objects suddenly flew from shelves and strange disturbances rippled through the rooms. Frightened guests called the police, but officers found no signs of forced entry or tampering. After they left, however, the disturbances returned, convincing many that something unearthly lingered in the house.

293. In December 1872, the merchant ship *Mary Celeste* was discovered adrift in the Atlantic Ocean, perfectly seaworthy but completely aban-

doned. A Canadian brig, the *Dei Gratia*, spotted her drifting near the Azores and sent a boarding party. Inside, they found the crew's belongings, cargo, and supplies untouched, with no evidence of a struggle or foul play. The ship's lifeboat was missing, but there were no clear signs of why the crew had left in such a hurry.

The mystery deepened when investigators confirmed that the *Mary Celeste* was fully stocked with food and water and had only minor damage, certainly not enough to force an evacuation. Over time, theories ranged from piracy and mutiny to waterspouts, sudden storms, and even paranormal explanations. But no definitive answers ever emerged.

294. On October 10, 2023, in Bakersfield, California, a routine traffic stop took a bizarre turn when the driver's passenger, a woman identified only as Sarah, suddenly vanished. Dashcam footage showed her sitting in the car one moment and gone the next — without a door opening or anyone nearby. Police searched the area but found no trace of her, and her identity could never be verified, leaving the disappearance an unsolved mystery.

295. The 1897 Greenbrier Ghost case is the only U.S. murder conviction said to have been guided by a ghost's testimony. After Elva Zona Shue's sudden death, her mother reported a visit from her daughter's spirit, revealing that her husband had strangled her. An autopsy confirmed strangulation, and the husband was convicted and sentenced to life.

296. A man selling cemetery plots once visited an elderly woman named Tilly, who paid him in cash taken from a soot-covered coffee can inside a spotless farmhouse. Weeks later, when he returned to finish paperwork, the home had vanished — reduced to ruins with its foundation stained black with soot. Locals told him the land had been abandoned for decades.

297. In 1916, 2 Philadelphia families abandoned their home after repeated encounters with a corpse-like apparition. Each night at 2 a.m., the figure appeared with glassy eyes and a rattling cough, gazing into a mirror before vanishing when the lights were switched on. The women were so terrified they fled immediately, while neighbors confirmed the house had long been rumored to be haunted after a young man died there

of tuberculosis. Witnesses said the ghost's presence grew stronger around Halloween, sealing the families' decision never to return.

298. Waverly Hills Sanatorium in Kentucky, once a tuberculosis hospital with thousands of deaths, is now infamous for ghost sightings. Visitors and paranormal investigators have captured photos of shadowy figures and apparitions, adding to its reputation as one of America's most haunted locations.

299. On a quiet night patrol in rural New Mexico, a police officer felt his cruiser jolt as if it had struck something in the road. He backed up, heart pounding, but the street lay empty. Hours later, reviewing the dashcam, he froze — the footage showed his car colliding with a shadowy, translucent figure that vanished on impact.

300. In a hotel in Illinois, guests repeatedly reported screaming from Room 209, despite no one being checked in. When the security manager entered the room, he found the furniture overturned, the carpet ripped up, and the shower running. A shadowy figure was seen exiting as he stepped inside. Some believed it was a spirit — or perhaps multiple entities — haunting the room.

301. In Ellicott City, Maryland, people claim to see the "Blink Man," a tall, thin figure with glowing red eyes that blink rapidly, often appearing before disasters.

302. Locals in Johnstown, Pennsylvania, reported seeing a ghost cow with no head and glowing eyes near an abandoned slaughterhouse. Witnesses described it floating, mooing from its neck stump, and even following fences before disappearing. The story dates back to an 1896 newspaper and is one of the strangest animal hauntings on record.

303. The Berini family's New England home grew quieter just before the footsteps began. A small boy in white would appear in the upstairs hall, pacing as if searching for someone, then stop to ask the same aching question every time: "Where do all the lonely people go?" His visits never came alone. Soon after, disembodied voices threaded through the rooms, objects shifted places, and doors nudged open as if by an unseen hand.

One night, the disturbance turned physical. The family watched the hallway rug ripple and lift at one corner, as though something beneath it were trying to get out. When they pulled it back, floorboards pried up easily, revealing a small medallion hidden in the dark space below — an object no one recognized but which felt like the answer to a riddle the boy couldn't speak. After that, the house never lost the sense that someone young and lonely still walked the hall, asking a question only the living could hear.

304. Entjen Gillis, a Dutch midwife during the Roermond witch trials of 1613, was accused of killing infants and performing unauthorized abortions. She confessed under torture and was executed.

305. In 1906, the Furnace Mill farmhouse in Lamberhurst became notorious for a string of unexplained disturbances. Horses were mysteriously moved between locked stalls, barrels were hurled down staircases, and doors opened on their own while the owner kept the only keys in his pocket. On one occasion, the farmer's son was found trapped inside a locked room, and locks and fasteners were seen shifting without human touch. Even under close watch, animals somehow appeared in sealed spaces. Police investigations offered no answers, leaving locals convinced the farmhouse was haunted.

306. In 1928, tenants of a Chester, Pennsylvania, boarding house claimed they were terrorized by a bizarre creature. They described it as bright red, with small horns and an insect-like buzzing that filled the room. In panic, they struck it with a chair and threw it out the window, after which it vanished. Locals whispered that the previous tenant, an elderly woman known for locking rooms in the house, had been trying to confine something dark and dangerous within its walls.

307. In 1965, in Asheville, North Carolina, Hedy Frederickson painted a ghostly figure from her recurring dreams, but the canvas soon changed — its blank features slowly filled in with the face of a man she had never imagined. The couple's house was plagued by eerie noises, sudden cold spots, and even bricked-up hidden rooms that added to the mystery. Word spread quickly, drawing hundreds of curious visitors, until the attention and disturbances grew so overwhelming that the Fredericksons were forced to move.

308. In 1927, a family in Fernvale, Australia, reported strange lights in the sky, mutilated livestock, and sightings of massive birds larger than eagles. Their ordeal climaxed when they encountered a humanoid figure dressed in a white suit before the disturbances abruptly ended. Investigators found scorched grass, odd feathers, and boot prints left behind. Locals remain divided over whether it was a UFO encounter or an unknown cryptid.

309. On July 8, 2023, in rural Montana, body cam footage captured an officer investigating strange noises at an abandoned location called Site 422. As he searched the eerie building, shadows moved in the windows, and chilling sounds echoed in the distance. He repeatedly mentioned seeing things he couldn't explain.

310. While on night patrol in the outskirts of Eureka, California, Officer Ben Malik noticed a woman crouched by the roadside as though trying to start a fire. As he approached, he was shocked to see her face flickering as if it were burning, and her behavior resembled a strange ritual. He eventually arrested her, but the encounter left him with more questions than answers. What exactly happened that night has never been explained.

311. On a 2017 episode of the British talk show *This Morning*, a supposedly haunted doll named "Scarlett" appeared to rock gently in its chair without being touched. The unsettling moment, captured on live TV, spooked the hosts and sparked a wave of speculation and debate among viewers about whether it was paranormal activity or a setup.

312. In 2007, a family in Puerto Montt, Chile, reported shadows moving through their home and cries warning them to leave. Police arrived to find shattered windows and household objects hurled outside. During the search, a ladder crashed down from the attic, and later footage revealed a dark figure shifting through the rooms. The police offered the terrified family shelter for the night.

313. On November 16, 2017, Julie and her daughter were driving a rural road in Maine when a massive buck suddenly leapt in front of their car. They felt the jarring impact, saw the deer strike the vehicle, and pulled over, bracing for wreckage. Yet the car was spotless — no dents, no scratches, no blood. Game wardens scoured the area but found no deer,

leaving Julie and her daughter shaken, both insisting they had seen and heard the collision that seemingly never happened.

314. In 1963, four children in Saskatchewan reported seeing a UFO release a glowing box, from which emerged a translucent figure about 10 feet tall (3 meters) dressed in monk-like robes. The being stretched out its arms, moaned, and drifted toward them, driving the children to flee in terror. One girl was so traumatized that she had to be hospitalized. Adults and police took the account seriously, especially since other UFOs were spotted nearby the same night. The rare mix of a UFO encounter with a ghostly apparition remains one of the strangest cases on record.

315. A hospital security officer in Chile working the night shift began recording strange and inexplicable events. Doors opened on their own, noises filled the halls, and shadows darted through empty rooms. Despite investigations, no one has been able to explain the occurrences. The hospital remains one of the country's most active paranormal hotspots.

316. Out in the desert near Marfa, Texas, folks have been seeing strange lights dancing on the horizon since 1883. They appear as glowing orbs — sometimes white, sometimes red or blue — that drift, split apart, or vanish without warning. Skeptics say they're just car headlights or heat waves, but locals swear some of the lights move in ways no vehicle or mirage ever could. Even scientists who studied them admitted a few sightings defy explanation.

317. One of the most unsettling "ghost photos" ever circulated is known as the Cooper family photo. Taken in the 1950s, it appears to show a family gathered in their living room, smiling for the camera — but hanging upside down in the background is a dark, shadowy figure resembling a human body. The image shocked viewers because no one present recalled seeing anything unusual when the picture was taken.

318. A 10-year-old girl in Virginia wandered off during a trip to a hidden creek and spent more than 8 hours lost in the woods. She heard footsteps echoing her own, then stumbled upon an unsettling clearing littered with old bathroom fixtures swallowed by vines. Later, she looked up to see a swirling black cloud overhead, ringing with the sound of church bells that

filled her with dread. She finally escaped when she reached a fence, only to discover no one had even realized she was missing.

319. In the early hours of March 3, 2021, at an industrial facility in Youngstown, Ohio, security cameras recorded a guard on a routine patrol when, without warning, he was hurled to the ground by an unseen force. The blow looked so sudden and violent that it seemed something invisible had attacked him, though the hallway was empty. The unsettling footage quickly spread, sparking paranormal speculation and leaving the incident shrouded in mystery.

320. On the night of June 18, 2022, in downtown St. Louis, Missouri, an off-duty officer leaving a parking garage was startled by strange noises echoing in the shadows. When he aimed his motorcycle light, it illuminated a figure strolling casually through the restricted area — where no one else should have been. The officer searched the entire garage but found nothing, and the mysterious figure was never identified.

321. While spending time at a quiet park in Japan, a man began receiving calls from a restricted number. At first, he dismissed them as a prank — until the caller, a young-sounding girl, began describing his exact situation. She detailed his clothing, where he was sitting, and even what he was doing, despite him never revealing his location. The realization hit hard: whoever was on the other end of the line was watching him in real time.

Then the caller's tone shifted. She claimed she was walking toward him from the open field nearby. The group scanned the area, but no one was there. Fear mounting, they grabbed their things and left the park immediately, shaken by the unseen presence. Later, the man discovered the park's dark history: years earlier, it had been the scene of a brutal murder. The phone calls, paired with the park's past, left him wondering if what he encountered that night was a cruel stalker's game — or something far more unsettling.

322. On November 1, 2014, a woman delivering newspapers at 4:30 a.m. in Minneapolis encountered 6 children in gray robes blocking the road. One girl walked toward her speaking gibberish, and the others fanned out to surround her car. Panicked, she drove onto a lawn to escape and then tried to follow them, but they vanished instantly. There were no houses

nearby, and no time for them to have disappeared. The encounter left her deeply disturbed, especially since it occurred just hours after Halloween.

323. In Madrid, Spain, in the summer of 2019, officer Carr Romero saw what he described as a ghost on surveillance cameras — something with legs, walking like a person, but not human. The entity walked through locked areas as if walls didn't exist. Detectives confirmed it wasn't a bug, camera glitch, or lighting issue.

324. In the 1950s, John May moved into a house near Lincoln, England, to prepare it for new owners, only to face disturbing phenomena. A candle lifted from its holder and rolled across the floor, and pages in his book turned rapidly as if by unseen hands. Locals said the house had belonged to a reclusive old woman who never left. After a quiet exorcism, the activity stopped, and the new owners were never told of its haunted past.

325. Late one night in October 2020, at a manufacturing plant in Gary, Indiana, a night shift worker stepped out for a smoke break behind the facility and saw someone near the fence. He radioed security but was told no one appeared on camera. Moments later, a figure charged at him from the dark, forcing him to flee inside and hold the door shut as the knob twisted violently. Surveillance footage showed no intruder but did capture the door handle moving on its own. Though no one talked about it afterward, several employees quietly began avoiding that part of the building at night.

326. In the winter of 2016, at a distribution center outside Toledo, Ohio, a man named Tim worked nights as a security guard, but his shifts became the stuff of nightmares. On one occasion, he noticed a pair of pale, bare feet standing just behind a locked door — feet that vanished when he opened it. Another night, a door he knew was secured swung open by itself, accompanied by a guttural roar that echoed through the halls.

Things escalated in the warehouse, where he saw long, shadowy arms stretching out of the darkness toward him. Later, in another corner of the building, he spotted a silent woman watching him, unmoving, her eyes fixed in the gloom. Moments later, his security footage cut out. That was the final straw — Tim walked away from the job and never returned.

327. In El Paso, a man twice witnessed commercial planes flying silently at low altitude over his backyard. Each time, he braced for a crash, but the planes simply vanished without sound or trace, and no reports ever surfaced. He later concluded he may have seen something bleeding through from another dimension.

328. Late one night in February 2022, at a shopping mall in Orlando, Florida, a security guard patrolling the food court followed the sound of a young girl crying. He discovered a child who said she was lost and searching for her mother, but when he reported it, fellow guards rushed to help and found the area empty. The girl had vanished without a trace, leaving the guard to wonder if she had ever been there at all.

329. In the spring of 1974, a quiet neighborhood in Culver City, California, became the epicenter of a chilling mystery. It began in a small home with knocks, cold spots, and drifting clouds of light that seemed to breathe. Then the activity turned violent. A mother reported being attacked by something she couldn't see, an unseen weight pinning her to the bed, a presence that left bruises and terror in its wake. Word reached a team of parapsychology researchers at the University of California, Los Angeles, who arrived with cameras, meters, and a plan to catch the haunting in the act.

During late-night séances, witnesses described a faceless torso coalescing out of a glowing mist, as if a body were trying to assemble itself from air. Photographs captured odd orbs, streaks, and warped patches of light, nothing like a face, but not quite nothing either. One investigator said the force pressed on his chest until he couldn't draw breath, a suffocation that lifted only when the room lights snapped on. The family fled the house, but the mother insisted the entity followed. She later claimed the presence had left her pregnant, a final, unsettling twist that ensured the case would be whispered about for decades. Whether nightmare, mass suggestion, or something that defies language, the "Entity" case still lingers, a story of a house where the dark seemed to learn a shape.

330. A boy in Pennsylvania consistently saw human-shaped shadows flickering at the edge of his vision, which seemed to follow him throughout the house.

331. The Battle of Edgehill in 1642, the first major clash of the English Civil War, gained eerie fame when locals reported ghostly soldiers refighting the battle in the skies above. Witnesses claimed to recognize the apparitions by name, and the haunting became so persistent that King Charles I ordered a royal commission to investigate — making it the only ghost sighting officially acknowledged by the British government. Believing the specters were a sign of divine punishment for the unburied dead, villagers began burying the fallen to bring peace.

332. In 1917, after a snowstorm in Greensburg, Kansas, townspeople witnessed a glowing angel in the sky, which was reportedly photographed. Many interpreted it as a spiritual visitation, with one man believing it was his deceased mother. Though the original paper didn't print the photo, scans exist, and the event remains part of local lore.

333. In Brazil, police were once called to an abandoned school after neighbors complained of eerie noises echoing through the halls. Once inside, they witnessed doors swinging open and slamming shut violently, even though the building was empty. Shaken by the unexplained activity, the officers cut their investigation short and left the site, unsettled by what they had encountered.

334. In Ojai, California, legends tell of the "Charman," a horribly burned man who roams back roads and canyons, carrying a lantern or reeking of smoke and burnt flesh.

335. Orbs are a staple of paranormal photography — glowing, translucent spheres that appear in pictures or videos, often hovering in midair. Believers see them as signs of spirits in motion, the souls of humans or animals traveling between realms. In ghost lore, orbs are sometimes considered the earliest stage of a haunting, with these floating lights acting as the precursor to a full-bodied apparition.

Skeptics, however, argue that most orbs are simply dust, pollen, or moisture reflecting a camera's flash. Still, countless ghost hunters treat them as spiritual evidence, claiming patterns in their brightness, color, or movement can reveal a presence. Whether dismissed as a photographic glitch or embraced as proof of life after death, orbs remain one of the most widely reported (and hotly debated) phenomena in paranormal investigation.

336. During a 2014 live soccer broadcast in Bolivia, viewers noticed a shadowy figure sprinting through the stands at high speed. The figure appeared to pass through seats and barriers without obstruction, fueling viral speculation about ghosts — though skeptics chalked it up to camera angles and optical illusion.

337. In Gettysburg, Pennsylvania, visitors have reported whispers, echoes of gunfire, mournful cries, and apparitions of soldiers from the Civil War battlefield.

338. On December 29, 2020, at a hotel in Chile, a security guard reported terrifying events following the death of a guest. While patrolling a stairwell, he heard faint footsteps that quickly escalated into the sound of someone sprinting up behind him, though no one was there. Panicked, he fled, later insisting that video footage showed a presence lurking behind a door. The incidents remained unexplained, adding to the hotel's eerie reputation.

339. In Eastern Kentucky, a teenager named Ben once encountered 2 strange men standing silently on a remote dirt road where no one should've been. They asked how he'd gotten past a gate that hadn't existed in years and stared at him with unsettling intensity. After walking away, Ben turned back and found the men had vanished from the straight, flat road with no place to hide. He ran home in a panic, convinced they weren't human.

7. Viral Madness & Online Insanity

The internet thrives on the strange, the eerie, and the inexplicable. From viral disappearances and mysterious videos to cryptic online art projects, the digital world is a playground for obsession, paranoia, and urban legend.

340. In April 2020, a chilling post appeared on Reddit from an 18-year-old who suspected his girlfriend and her sister were secretly poisoning him. For months, he had suffered unexplained stomach pain, vomiting, and illness that seemed to follow meals they prepared. He described how they insisted he only eat food they made, discouraged him from cooking for himself, and even exchanged texts whenever his symptoms flared.

Other Redditors urged him to take precautions, suggesting tricks like swapping plates, preparing his own meals, or seeing a doctor to rule out serious medical conditions. The thread quickly filled with speculation, some convinced he was being poisoned, others pointing toward a severe gastrointestinal disorder. But after that night, the original poster never returned with an update. His account went silent, leaving the community with no closure. To this day, no one knows whether the young man uncovered a sinister plot, discovered a hidden illness, or simply disappeared into anonymity.

341. Hiker Kenny Veach claimed to have found a cave in Nevada near Nellis Air Force Base that made his body vibrate. After announcing plans to revisit, he disappeared in 2014. His phone was found near an abandoned mine, but his body was never recovered.

342. In the 1990s, a Mexican TV station aired missing-person alerts, one featuring 18-year-old Selene Delgado Lopez. Viewers claimed her photo froze their TVs, and later found no records of her disappearance. Theories grew that her face was fabricated, possibly tied to a police sketch of a serial killer, cementing her as an urban legend.

343. In 2023, TikTok videos of a 35-year-old Chinese woman named Xia Xia, who appeared childlike due to a rare condition, went viral. Clips showed her lashing out at people, sparking memes and Halloween

costumes. Later, her accounts were banned amid allegations of parental exploitation, though officials insisted she wasn't abused.

344. Hitogata is a rumored Japanese commercial that shows 2 figures near train tracks with eerie audio. No copy has ever been verified, though recreations exist.

345. October28,2011.com was a website filled with cryptic images, music, and downloads. It went offline in 2015, but archives show disturbing and incoherent content with hidden files.

346. Unfavorable Semicircle was a YouTube channel that began uploading in 2015 and quickly gained attention for its surreal, minimalist videos. Most lasted just a few seconds and featured a single pixel, static backgrounds, or a distorted voice reading a number or letter. All the titles included a Sagittarius symbol, adding another layer of cryptic intent. The channel was terminated in early 2016 without explanation, sparking even more speculation.

Redditors attempted to decode the videos by creating composites — layered images from frames — to find patterns or hidden visuals. Some of these even included 3D graph interpretations based on color data from each frame. In 2022, a Twitter account linked to the project resurfaced and posted cryptic messages, images, and links referencing alien communication, outsider art, and the Voyager Golden Record. The creator later admitted it was an experimental stream-of-consciousness art project inspired by Webdriver Torso, designed to test how far viewers would go to solve something so abstract.

347. In the late 1980s, dialing 1-800-GOLF-TIP in Canada led not to golf advice but to a man counting, followed by a piercing siren sound. The strange number appeared on billboards and intrigued thousands until it was revealed to have been linked to PGA promotions, then acquired by Mayfair Communications, which bizarrely turned it into an adult hotline in the U.S. The odd detour still puzzles many.

348. By 2023, OnlyFans contributed over £1 billion annually to the U.K. economy through taxes, tech employment, and creator income, maintaining dominance over rivals like Fansly and LoyalFans.

349. In 1994, a mysterious poster called "Publius" jumped onto alt.music.pink-floyd, claiming The Division Bell hid a riddle with a real prize. Clues spilled online, and at a New Jersey show, the stage lights even flashed ENIGMA PUBLIUS, which poured gasoline on the hunt. No winner ever stepped forward, and no official "solution" was announced. Years later, David Gilmour waved it off as a record-company stunt, and drummer Nick Mason likewise pinned it on the label.

350. A Reddit user known as "yay video games" spent years posting incoherent messages about DRM and Ubisoft, occasionally mixing in normal comments. Later, it emerged he had been living with chronic illness and mental health challenges. He died by suicide in 2015.

351. The Most Mysterious Song on the Internet is an unidentified 1980s metal track recorded from a German radio broadcast. Despite decades of searching, its origin and artist remain unknown.

352. In 2015, an American man in Japan named James R. launched a campaign claiming his son had been left in a vegetative state by rogue doctors. His YouTube videos mixed medical accusations with conspiracy theories about immortality and stem cells. Many believe his son suffers from a genetic condition, and James fabricated the rest.

353. On November 22, 1987, Chicago viewers witnessed one of the strangest broadcast intrusions in television history. During an evening news program on WGN, the screen suddenly flickered to a figure in a rubbery Max Headroom mask, a distorted version of the 1980s TV character. That first signal was cut within seconds, but later that night, a PBS affiliate airing *Doctor Who* was hijacked again. This time, the masked figure lasted over a minute on air, babbling in garbled speech, grunting, and even brandishing a flyswatter in a bizarre whipping gesture.

Investigators determined the pirate had used a powerful microwave transmission to exploit the "capture effect," a loophole where a stronger broadcast signal overrides a weaker one. Pulling such an operation off required not just expensive gear but also significant technical knowledge, leading some to suspect the culprit might have been an insider familiar with the stations' systems. The FBI and the Federal Communications Commission opened investigations, but no suspect was ever caught.

Five years later, the statute of limitations expired, meaning the masked hijacker could never face prosecution even if unmasked. Decades on, the "Max Headroom incident" remains unsolved — a surreal act of media sabotage that turned a night of local TV into an enduring piece of broadcast folklore.

354. A 4chan user robbed a bank in 2015 after announcing his plan online, even posting photos of the stolen cash. He kept updating the thread while hiding in a hotel, but was arrested 2 weeks later. Identified as Pedro Smith, he received just 3 years in prison despite using a fake gun. Later, he was found living in a $1.5 million home.

355. In 2013, a YouTube channel called Webdriver Torso started uploading thousands of short videos featuring red and blue rectangles on a white background. These were accompanied by high-pitched beeping sounds, and each video lasted about a second. The bizarre nature of the uploads led to wild theories involving spies, aliens, and secret codes. Eventually, Google admitted it was an internal testing tool for checking YouTube's video compression quality.

356. In 2014, a 4chan user posted corrupt files after claiming their friend had downloaded a virus. When pieced together, the images formed a demonic red face with the words "I Am God." Those who opened it later reported paranormal activity, from lights switching off to figures in their homes. The original poster vanished, leaving the thread to die without answers.

357. Elisa Lam, a Canadian student, disappeared in Los Angeles in 2013 while staying at the Cecil Hotel. Disturbing elevator footage showed her acting erratically. Weeks later, her body was found in the hotel's rooftop water tank. Her death was ruled accidental drowning, but how she accessed the roof remains mysterious.

358. The website 973-Namuh-973.com features endless numerology puzzles, religious symbolism, and cryptic mazes. Users claim it hides secret truths but often report paranoia after studying it.

359. A U.S. World of Warcraft player living in Japan disappeared after the 2011 Tōhoku earthquake and tsunami, and was never heard from again.

His online friends mourned his absence, but no official confirmation of his fate was ever found.

360. In the virtual world *Second Life*, a player using their real surname was reportedly invited by 2 strangers to a strange in-game house. Once inside, one of them revealed they had researched the player's real identity and threatened to post screenshots of the encounter on their Facebook. The incident blurred the line between online roleplay and real-life harassment, leaving the player deeply unsettled.

361. In 2015, a YouTube channel called Obscure Horror Corner uploaded a four-part playthrough of a strange game known only as Sad Satan. The footage showed the player wandering through endless black-and-white hallways filled with distorted audio and unsettling imagery. At random moments, real photographs would flash onscreen — including infamous figures like Jimmy Savile, who was later exposed for horrific crimes. There were no clear objectives, only the sense of walking deeper into something designed to unsettle.

According to the uploader, the game came from a hidden corner of the dark web and even included a cryptic text file. After facing backlash, the creator claimed to have deleted it, but not before a corrupted copy surfaced on 4chan. That version was laced with malware and disturbingly illegal content, including gore and child exploitation material (known in internet slang as "cheese pizza"). Whether this was a malicious clone or a modified update of the original remains unknown.

Reddit users eventually built a "clean" version of Sad Satan, stripped of harmful code and illegal files, but the damage to the game's reputation lingered. Nearly a decade later, no one has definitively identified who made the game or what purpose it was meant to serve. Sad Satan endures as one of the internet's most chilling gaming mysteries — a creation caught somewhere between art project, urban legend, and nightmare.

362. A group of Xbox players met a man in *GTA V* who pretended to talk to his wife and kids through voice chat, complete with fake sound effects. When questioned, he got defensive and abruptly disappeared, never logging on again.

363. In 2021, a video went viral of a bloodied, pale woman, limping and screaming in Seattle, quickly dubbed the "Seattle Zombie Woman." Police responded but offered no details, fueling theories from violent crime to possession. Later, bodycam footage revealed it was an elaborate stunt using theatrical makeup, staged by activist Kimberly Casi, but its disturbing realism left a lasting impression.

364. John Lang, a Fresno activist, claimed police were harassing him and trying to frame him. He posted evidence and warnings online. In 2016, he was found dead in his burned home with stab wounds. His death was ruled a suicide, but many suspect foul play.

365. A female gamer playing *Modern Warfare 3* was stalked by a player named Kevin who became obsessed with her voice, offered to buy her games, begged for voice clips, and turned aggressive when rejected.

366. After a 2008 Los Angeles train crash, Charles Peck's cell phone made 35 calls to loved ones over 11 hours. He had died on impact, and his phone was never found, leading to speculation about paranormal activity or malfunctions.

367. In 2019, a 750-page book titled *Around the World in 2,000 Pictures* surfaced in South Carolina, filled with cryptic codes, maps, coordinates, and esoteric symbols scribbled alongside normal photos. References to Freemasonry, Cherokee language, and hidden websites suggested a larger puzzle called "50 Joanna." Despite links to obscure YouTube videos and maps pointing to sites across the U.S. and U.K., no one has solved it.

368. Chris-Chan, later known as Christine Weston Chandler, became one of the internet's most documented figures after creating the Sonichu comics. His odd artwork, interactions with trolls, and increasingly erratic videos drew worldwide attention. In 2021, Chris was arrested for incest with his mother, cementing his place as one of the most infamous internet personalities of all time.

369. In 2008, a man uploaded a video claiming he had been high for 2 months straight after boiling the roots of an unknown hallucinogen. Slurring and distressed, he suggested it might have been datura. The video vanished, and he was never identified, leaving only speculation about whether it was real or staged.

370. In 1996, a strange phenomenon gripped Usenet forums when hundreds of posts appeared under the same puzzling subject line: "Markovian Parallax Denigrate." The messages were incoherent, filled with strings of random words that had no obvious meaning or pattern. Amateur codebreakers and conspiracy theorists alike tried to make sense of the bizarre texts, speculating that they might conceal a hidden cipher or encrypted instructions. Yet despite decades of effort, no one has managed to prove that a message was ever buried in the nonsense.

The mystery grew sharper when the posts were traced back to an account tied to Susan Lindauer, a former journalist who years later would be arrested for acting as an unregistered foreign agent. When contacted, Lindauer flatly denied any involvement, insisting she had nothing to do with the infamous posts. That denial left researchers with even more questions. Were the messages part of a failed experiment, an elaborate prank, or something more clandestine? Nearly 30 years on, the "Markovian Parallax Denigrate" files remain one of the strangest unsolved riddles of the early internet.

The term "Markovian" may refer to the Markov process, a statistical model used in many modern technologies, including search engines and AI chatbots. Some people theorized the posts were generated by an early form of automated AI text or were part of a research experiment. However, nothing has ever been proven. The gibberish remains one of the internet's oldest and strangest linguistic mysteries.

371. Mariana's Web is a myth about the deepest level of the internet, supposedly accessible only with quantum computing. It's said to contain government secrets, historical archives, and forbidden knowledge.

372. In 2021, Instagram accounts like "TruthSticks11" and "SmartSchoolBoy9" appeared, run by a man dressed as a schoolchild with white makeup and red lipstick. He followed children's accounts and posted unsettling playground videos. Sleuths identified him as a 59-year-old London man named David Alter, now under police scrutiny.

373. In 2008, 4chan users attacked the Epilepsy Foundation's forum by posting flashing GIFs designed to trigger seizures. Several people suffered migraines and full seizures. The attackers were never caught.

374. A college student allowed a stranger named Chris — met in a voice chatroom — to remotely access his laptop to fix a minor issue. Later that night, he awoke at 3:30 a.m. to find the laptop mysteriously powered on, displaying webcam photos of his empty room, then one of himself, and finally an image of the outside of his house. As his dog barked violently downstairs, he panicked, fled to a hotel, and eventually burned the laptop, never speaking to Chris again. The true extent of the breach was never discovered, but he believed someone had been watching him through the machine.

375. In the 1928 film *The Circus*, a woman appears to hold an object resembling a cellphone. Explanations include an early hearing aid, though some claim it shows a time traveler.

376. In 2010, a man created the YouTube channel "I'm Seeing Gnomes" to show supposed footage of tiny creatures in his backyard. He posted videos of tracks, noises, and eerie movement outside his home, as well as blog updates. His last entry, ominously titled "The Next Step," appeared in May 2010 before he vanished from the internet, leaving the mystery unresolved.

377. The image of Jeff the Killer became infamous in creepypasta lore around 2008, showing a pale face with huge eyes and a carved smile. The origins of the photo are disputed — rumored to be a bullied girl who killed herself, a photoshopped forum post, or an early internet hoax — but none of the stories have been verified. Its unsettling ambiguity has made it a permanent internet mystery.

378. DicksByMail.com lets users anonymously mail gummy "body part" candies with a message to people they dislike.

379. In 2011, a mysterious Reddit account named A858D45F56D9BC9 began filling its own subreddit with long, 64-character strings of encrypted text. At first glance, the posts looked like gibberish, but curious users began decoding them and found strange surprises — one message simply read "Thank you for the gold," another dropped the random word "Maverick" alongside a photo of Sarah Palin. The randomness fueled endless speculation: was it a bot experiment, an art project, or something more sinister?

The mystery deepened in 2015 when the user appeared for an Ask Me Anything and gave only a cryptic response: "We cannot disclose the purpose." No further explanation was offered, and the posts stopped the following year. Later, the creators hinted that a woman had managed to solve part of the puzzle but admitted that the rest would stay unsolved because "the public information is insufficient." More than a decade later, the A858 subreddit remains one of Reddit's strangest unsolved mysteries, a puzzle whose answers may never fully be revealed.

380. In the Paris Catacombs, an unsettling video surfaced showing a man wandering the labyrinth of tunnels before becoming disoriented and panicked. He drops his camera and flees into the darkness, with the footage ending abruptly. The explorer was never identified, and the eerie tape remains a source of speculation and urban legend.

381. In 2010, a 4chan "experiment" urged users to heat a duct-taped spoon and cool it rapidly, causing it to explode. Dozens were injured by metal shrapnel. The prank spread to other sites before fading from public view.

382. Two boys using Omegle typed in their hometown as an interest and connected with a user whose camera was black, but who sent them a suspicious link. The site appeared blank at first, but later began showing live footage of nearby streets, eventually revealing their exact neighborhood and finally one of the boys' homes. The camera entered their backyard, retrieved a hidden spare key, and attempted to enter the house. Terrified, the boys hid in the basement, heard someone trying the locked basement door, and eventually called the police — who found nothing stolen, except for the missing key.

383. "Erratas" is said to be a secret corporate surveillance program. Searching the word "allegedly" triggers monitoring. Associated YouTube videos contained hidden Morse code and strange captions, fueling belief in a cover-up.

384. In 2017, a Reddit user described watching a bizarre broadcast on Nickelodeon that showed naked, zombified humans marching into hamster wheels in a looping, bleak scene. The footage vanished moments later, replaced by a normal *SpongeBob* episode, and no trace of the video

was ever found. Other users recalled seeing the same thing, but theories like glitched commercials or TV hijackings didn't fully explain it. Whether a broadcast intrusion or a misremembered dream, the experience remains an unsettling, unsolved mystery.

385. Laughing Horse Orifice Headquarters is a bizarre website filled with flashing images, conspiracies, and hidden text. Its exact purpose remains unclear, but it is linked to online art and paranoia.

386. While playing an online dating sim with his cousin, a 13-year-old pretended to be female and discovered the stranger flirting with them lived just down the street. Creeped out, they logged off — seconds later, they heard gunshots and arguing.

387. A 26-minute VHS called *Grave Robbing for Morons* surfaced in the 1990s, showing a man named Anthony calmly explaining how to rob graves while handling what appeared to be a real skull. Whether genuine or staged, the disturbing footage circulated widely online, but Anthony's identity and the tape's true purpose remain unknown.

388. A disturbing photo called the "Monan Tunnels" showed 2 masked figures and what looked like a dead child in a field. Posted on 4chan in 2018, it sparked debate over whether it was real or staged. No source, metadata, or matching crime was ever found. Its origin remains a mystery.

389. In late 2024, Reddit user SuperHeatran2 stumbled upon something that seemed straight out of a horror movie prop bin: inside an old Kodak carousel box at a thrift store lay a single 35-millimeter slide. It depicted a blood-stained, possibly lifeless human body slumped between a bed and a wall — an image too realistic to dismiss as mere shock art.

Alarmed, the user contacted the police, who arrived swiftly, photographed the scene, and seized the image for forensic evaluation. Reddit sleuths speculated that the slide could have once belonged to a crime scene photographer or law enforcement insider — perhaps even part of old training files or evidence — now lost amid donated items.

Months passed with no official update, leaving the image's origin, and the fate it captured, shrouded in silence.

390. In 2017, a Redditor named FlipAndFlop announced he would try the deadly hallucinogenic plant datura, despite warnings. Hours later, his incoherent posts suggested he had taken it, after which he never returned to Reddit. Whether he died, abandoned the account, or staged the story remains unknown years later.

391. In 2008, a website called This Man claimed thousands of people had dreamed of the same face. It offered theories about his identity. It was later revealed to be part of a viral marketing campaign.

392. In 1997, radio host Howard Stern took a chilling call from a man identifying himself as "Clay," who claimed to be a serial killer in New Orleans targeting prostitutes. The caller shared disturbing details that reportedly matched aspects of unsolved cases, even suggesting the suspect was a Black police officer. Although a taxi driver was later convicted of some of the murders, "Clay's" true identity — and whether he was genuinely involved — has never been confirmed.

393. John Titor claimed in 2000 on the Time Travel Institute forum to be a soldier from 2036 sent to retrieve an IBM 5100 computer. He predicted civil war in 2005 and nuclear strikes on U.S. cities, none of which occurred. Debate continues on whether he was a hoaxer or part of an elaborate roleplay.

394. A 1964 photograph of a girl with an apparent spaceman behind her became known as the Solway Firth Spaceman. It was later shown that the figure was her mother with her back turned.

8. Freakish Bodies & Medical Nightmares

The human body is a wonder of evolution — strange, fragile, and sometimes horrifying. From glowing skin and disappearing bones to bizarre vulnerabilities under extreme conditions, the biology of humans teeters between awe and terror.

395. Yawning was once thought to increase oxygen supply to the brain. Newer theories suggest it may help cool the brain or serve as a social signal that synchronizes behavior within groups.

396. If your body catches on fire, your eyeballs will melt from their sockets before you lose consciousness, assuming you don't suffocate first — a horrifyingly vivid example of human vulnerability in extreme conditions.

397. People with psychotic disorders perceive auditory hallucinations differently across cultures, with U.S. patients reporting more hostile voices than those in Ghana or India.

398. Bones are living, dynamic tissue rich with blood vessels, and they're constantly breaking down and rebuilding through a process called remodeling. In fact, you essentially get a brand-new skeleton about every 10 years as old bone is replaced with new.

399. The human brain essentially named itself, becoming aware of its own existence and its ability to generate an endless stream of thought. This self-referential act makes it one of the most remarkable organs in nature.

400. Humans emit extremely faint visible light, about a thousand times dimmer than our eyes detect. The glow varies across the body and arises from metabolic reactions producing reactive oxygen species that sometimes generate photons — bioluminescence without evolutionary function.

401. Babies have around 300 bones; adults have 206. Many infant bones are cartilage-rich and pliable, aiding birth and early growth. With age, bones ossify and fuse — skull plates, spine segments, and hip elements merge — reducing the total adult count.

402. Rectal prolapse is a medical condition in which a portion of the intestine slips out through the anus, often due to chronic constipation, intense straining during bowel movements, or weakened pelvic muscles. It can cause discomfort, bleeding, and a visible bulge, and often requires medical treatment or surgery.

403. Your cornea stays clear by being bloodless. It pulls oxygen straight from the air when your eyes are open — and from tears and aqueous humor when they're closed — so nothing opaque gets in the way.

404. Male nipples serve no biological function related to feeding, and their presence is a leftover from early fetal development before the embryo's sex is fully determined.

405. Humans shed around 30,000 to 40,000 skin cells every minute, which adds up to over 4 million per day. Most of it becomes household dust.

406. Blushing occurs when tiny blood vessels in the face dilate, causing a rush of blood that reddens the skin — usually in response to embarrassment, shame, or social attention. While the physical mechanism is well understood, the evolutionary reason behind this involuntary and often awkward reaction is still unclear.

407. A bone marrow transplant doesn't just treat disease; it can rewrite your blood. Donor stem cells take over the factory floor of hematopoiesis, and the recipient's blood type can flip to match the donor's. Afterward, a cheek swab and a blood draw might tell 2 different DNA stories.

408. Your face is covered in microscopic mites called Demodex. They are invisible to the naked eye and impossible to completely remove, living undetected in hair follicles and pores.

409. It takes about the same force to rip off a human ear as it does to tear through 7 sheets of paper at once.

410. Everyone has a unique microbiome — a complex community of microbes that live in and on the body — but scientists still don't fully understand how these personalized ecosystems are formed and maintained. Factors like genetics, diet, environment, and even birth method all play a role, but the exact mechanisms remain a mystery.

411. Pruney fingers aren't caused by soaking up water. Submersion triggers nervous-system vasoconstriction, which reduces finger volume, causing the skin to fold into wrinkles. The adaptive purpose is debated; experiments suggest wrinkling doesn't improve grip on wet objects as once hypothesized.

412. There is a rare genetic disorder called fibrodysplasia ossificans progressiva, which causes injured tissue to transform into bone. Over time, new bone growth locks joints and traps the person inside a rigid "second skeleton," severely limiting movement.

413. The mouth hosts more than 700 species of bacteria, making it one of the dirtiest parts of the body — even dirtier than a toilet seat.

414. Straining too hard during a bowel movement can trigger the vagus nerve, slow your heart rate, drop your blood pressure, and cause you to faint — or in extreme cases, die.

415. Rod cells in your eyes are incredibly sensitive. In perfect conditions, they can respond to just one particle of light (a photon). At the limits of vision, your eyes are essentially counting individual light particles. In darkness, they act like tiny particle detectors, picking up the faintest glimmers.

416. Some human faces are perceived as "punchable" due to certain evolved facial traits — such as prominent brows, wider jaws, and flatter noses — that may have developed to better absorb impacts during physical confrontations. These features, once advantageous in ancient hand-to-hand combat, can now trigger subconscious social reactions in modern settings.

417. After your heart stops, your brain can stay alive for up to 5 minutes. During that time, you might gasp, twitch, or appear briefly conscious.

418. Laughter may be linked to social bonding and the release of feel-good chemicals in the brain, but it's unclear why we laugh when alone or at inappropriate times.

419. Some people carry blood that's almost mythical. Rh-null — nicknamed "golden blood" — lacks every Rh antigen and has been documented in only a few dozen individuals worldwide. It can save almost

anyone with rare Rh types, but finding a donor for them is a global scavenger hunt.

420. Unlike other mammals, human females retain large breasts even when not nursing. Some theories suggest this trait might attract mates or aid in fat storage for milk production, but there's no confirmed reason why human females have permanently enlarged breasts.

421. Humans lack hydroreceptors, so we don't "feel" wetness directly. Our brains infer wetness from coldness, texture, and pressure. That's why cold clothes can seem damp, or a chilly metal seat feels suspicious — our perception is an educated sensory guess.

422. Before modern medicine, people in deep comas or unconscious states were sometimes mistakenly buried alive. Some coffins were equipped with bells or breathing tubes to prevent this.

423. Anesthesia awareness is a rare condition where patients wake up during surgery but can't move or speak. They may feel pain, pressure, or hear everything around them without anyone knowing.

424. A gene called 5-HTT influences serotonin production, and individuals with 2 long versions tend to be significantly happier and more resilient.

425. The human bloodstream contains about 0.2 milligrams of gold. It serves no purpose but technically makes your body a little more valuable.

426. The brain has no pain receptors, so it can't feel anything directly. This is the reason patients can undergo brain surgery while awake.

427. The appendix is thought to play a role in immune function and maintaining healthy gut bacteria, particularly during early life. However, many people live perfectly well without it, and its original evolutionary purpose remains a topic of scientific debate.

428. Decomposition starts within minutes of death. Cells begin to break down, and bacteria start digesting tissues from the inside out.

429. Human hair displays a wide range of colors — from black and brown to blonde and red — primarily due to genetic variation in melanin production. However, the evolutionary reasons behind this diversity

remain unclear, with theories ranging from climate adaptation to sexual selection.

430. Modern humans are covered in body hair, yet it serves little purpose compared to the thick fur coats of our ancestors. Unlike other mammals, our sparse hair provides almost no protection from cold or heat, leaving scientists puzzled as to why it persists. Some theories suggest it plays a role in sensation, sexual selection, or parasite detection, but none fully explain why evolution didn't eliminate it entirely.

What's left is a biological relic: a faint reminder of our evolutionary past. Though it no longer regulates temperature or shields us from the elements, human body hair endures, an ancient feature whose exact purpose remains a mystery.

431. Cardiopulmonary resuscitation is highly unreliable; even if performed correctly, there is about an 88% chance it will fail, resulting in the person dying despite your best efforts.

432. Goosebumps occur in response to cold or fear, causing tiny muscles at the base of hair follicles to contract, a reaction that likely evolved to make our fur-covered ancestors appear larger or retain warmth, but in modern humans, it serves little practical purpose.

433. The liver is a biochemical powerhouse, quietly handling over 500 essential tasks. It detoxifies blood, produces bile for digestion, stores glycogen and iron, and synthesizes key proteins. Without it, the body's chemistry would fall apart.

434. Atoms are made up mostly of empty space. If you removed that emptiness from every human — compressing all atomic nuclei and electrons together — the entire human population could fit into the volume of a sugar cube. That's how dense matter becomes when you eliminate the gaps between atoms.

435. Studies estimate that the average person ingests about 0.18 ounces (5 grams) of microplastics each week — roughly the weight of a credit card. Researchers warn that this accumulation may trigger inflammation, disrupt hormones, and contribute to neurotoxicity over time.

436. Fingerprints are unique identifiers, but their functional purpose — if any — is debated. They were once thought to aid grip, though evidence for this is weak.

437. The organs in the human body naturally arrange themselves in the correct order during development, meaning surgeons typically don't need to reorganize them during procedures.

438. Sneezing with your mouth and nose closed can build up enough pressure to partially dislodge an eyeball. It's rare but possible, which is why doctors advise against holding in sneezes.

439. Teeth are the hardest substance in the body and don't decompose like soft tissue. They can survive long after death and help forensic teams identify remains.

440. When you smell something foul, tiny odor-carrying particles actually stick to the inside of your nose. That's how your brain detects scents, by physically interacting with microscopic molecules in the air.

441. The human body produces 1 to 2 quarts of mucus daily, most of which drains silently into your throat and is swallowed without notice.

442. Certain smells and tastes can evoke vivid emotions or memories, often more intensely than sights or sounds. While it's known that the brain's olfactory and gustatory systems are closely linked to emotional centers like the amygdala and hippocampus, the exact reason for this powerful connection remains unclear.

443. The chemical composition of human tissue is so similar to that of pigs that in blind taste tests, people often cannot distinguish between pork and human meat, highlighting a disturbing biological overlap.

444. Sleep is one of biology's great paradoxes. Every species studied so far requires it, suggesting it's essential for survival, yet it leaves creatures completely vulnerable — an odd trait in a world built on predator and prey. Scientists know that sleep plays a role in restoring the brain, repairing the body, and consolidating memories, but why it evolved in the first place remains a mystery.

Even after decades of research, no one can fully explain why every animal, from humans to jellyfish, must spend hours in this helpless state. Sleep is clearly critical — depriving the body of it leads to illness, cognitive decline, and eventually death — but its ultimate purpose remains an unanswered question, a universal ritual whose secrets are locked inside the mind itself.

445. In cases of extreme starvation, the body starts consuming brain tissue after fat and muscle run out, causing severe and lasting damage.

446. The heart can continue beating even outside the body if it's supplied with oxygen. It has its own electrical system, separate from the brain.

447. Babies develop fine body hair in the womb called lanugo, which may initially appear like a mustache and eventually spread to cover the whole body. Lanugo helps regulate body temperature and keep the infant warm before birth.

448. Blood types are one of medicine's most basic classifications, yet their origins remain mysterious. Scientists know that the 4 major types — A, B, AB, and O — are distributed unevenly around the world, with some populations showing strong patterns, such as a high prevalence of type O among Indigenous peoples of the Americas. Researchers believe these variations may have evolved in response to regional pressures like disease, diet, or environment, giving certain blood types an advantage in specific areas.

Despite these theories, no definitive explanation has emerged for why humans developed multiple blood types at all. A fundamental part of our biology remains an evolutionary puzzle, hinting that our blood still carries secrets from humanity's distant past.

449. Humans exhibit a wide variety of eye colors due to genetic differences affecting melanin levels in the iris.

450. Prions are misfolded proteins that cause fatal brain diseases by triggering other proteins to misfold, destroying brain tissue.

451. Your nose is far more discerning than we once thought — likely able to tell apart on the order of a trillion different odor mixtures. It's not just

one receptor at work, but a combinatorial orchestra firing unique patterns to the brain. Scent is high-dimensional data your mind reads in an instant.

452. Complex actions like typing rely on seamless coordination between the eyes, brain, and muscles. Yet even though understanding the basic pathways, scientists still don't fully grasp how the brain manages such precise, real-time control of movement.

453. The Mutter Museum in Philadelphia, Pennsylvania, displays preserved internal organs, anatomical models, and equipment used in biomedical research. It features disturbing mutations, tumors, and anomalies of human anatomy, making it both educational and unsettling.

454. Fatal familial insomnia is a genetic condition that destroys the sleep center of the brain, leading to hallucinations, loss of speech, and eventually death.

9. Hidden Scandals & Star Confessions

Behind the glitz, the story is darker. Stars, rulers, and nobles have indulged in wild habits, criminal acts, and shocking confessions — revealing that power and fame often come with a side of scandal.

455. Marlon Brando shocked Hollywood with his eccentric habits. He was known for devouring entire tubs of ice cream in one sitting and often ignored traditional acting rules. Despite his legendary performances, directors complained that he rarely memorized his lines, choosing instead to read them off cue cards because he believed it made his delivery feel more natural.

456. In 2011, Neil Patrick Harris and David Burtka served a Halloween meat platter styled as Amy Winehouse's corpse; after backlash years later, Harris apologized and called it "regrettable."

457. Empress Elizabeth of Russia, who reigned from 1741 to 1762, turned royal balls into gender-bending spectacles. She mandated that guests cross-dress, with men floundering under hoop skirts while she showed off her legs in breeches. It was part power play, part party, and fully on her terms.

458. Charlie Sheen's downfall became headline material. In 2011, he admitted to heavy spending on prostitutes and drugs, and delivered a now-infamous rant calling himself a "warlock" with "tiger blood" and boasting that he was "winning." His erratic behavior led to his firing from *Two and a Half Men*. Rather than backing down, he leaned into the chaos, using it as part of his public persona.

459. Metta World Peace, formerly known as Ron Artest, once damaged a $100,000 TV camera in frustration after a game at Madison Square Garden. In another moment of unpredictability, he took a job at Circuit City solely for the employee discount and quit after one shift. His career often blended moments of volatility with an ongoing effort to find personal growth and stability.

460. After the 1981 assassination attempt on Ronald Reagan, his wife, Nancy Reagan, turned to astrology for guidance. She began consulting an

astrologer — never meeting her directly, but relying on an intermediary to relay information. Presidential schedules were quietly shaped by the stars.

461. Chris Brown's brutal assault on Rihanna in 2009 made headlines worldwide, but it wasn't the end of his history with violence. Years later, his ex-girlfriend Karrueche Tran was granted a five-year restraining order against him after testifying that he had threatened her and been physically abusive during their relationship. Other women have come forward with allegations of violence and intimidation, painting a picture of repeated abuse that has followed Brown throughout his career.

Despite this, Brown's music career has remained largely unaffected. He continues to release chart-topping songs, collaborate with major artists, and win awards, often performing on some of the industry's biggest stages.

462. Countess Elizabeth Báthory, a noblewoman with royal blood who lived from 1560 to 1614, was accused of torturing and killing scores of young girls. She allegedly believed bathing in their blood would preserve her youth. When the crimes came to light, she was sealed into a windowless room, where she died in isolation.

463. Crown Prince Sado of Korea, who lived from 1735 to 1762, unraveled into violence and delusion, reportedly killing servants and attacking palace staff. His father, King Yeongjo, ordered an unthinkable punishment: Sado was locked inside a rice chest, where he died over 8 agonizing days. The court whispered about his crimes long after his death.

464. President Kennedy's wife, Jackie Kennedy, and her sister, Lee Radziwill, had a long-standing rivalry shaped by social status and personal relationships. Their tensions deepened when Jackie married Aristotle Onassis, who had previously been romantically involved with Lee, reportedly without informing her beforehand. The strain between them persisted, and when Jackie passed away, she left nothing to Lee in her will.

465. Clark Gable kept a carefully groomed image but had quirks few expected. He shaved his chest and armpits, avoided baths, and used a portable shower in the army. Vivien Leigh famously complained about his breath — but he couldn't have cared less.

466. Elizabeth Taylor's love life became as famous as her films. Married eight times, she openly admitted that some of her marriages were mistakes and that she rushed into love more than once. Her struggles with pills and alcohol led to several stays in rehab, yet she remained unembarrassed about her past, often speaking honestly about her battles and her determination to recover.

467. Daryl Dawkins smashed backboards and gave his dunks names like "Yo-Mama" and "Spine-Chiller Supreme." He claimed to be from the planet Lovetron, sent to Earth to spread "interplanetary funkmanship." The NBA eventually had to redesign its rims just to contain him.

468. Bill Cosby was accused by dozens of women of drugging and sexual assault over several decades. In 2018, he was convicted of aggravated indecent assault and sentenced to prison. However, in 2021, the conviction was overturned by the Pennsylvania Supreme Court due to a violation of his due process rights. Although released from prison, Cosby remains widely discredited in the public eye.

469. When Christina Crawford published *Mommie Dearest*, she imagined Joan Crawford as a volatile, image-obsessed disciplinarian rather than a flawless star. The memoir's emblematic moment — Joan erupting over "no wire hangers," striking Christina with one, then forcing a late-night scrub of the closet — became shorthand for a home ruled by appearances and fear. The portrait was explosive, turning a Hollywood icon into a figure of fear and sparking public arguments about what really happened behind closed doors.

The backlash was immediate and lasting: friends and colleagues defended Joan, others backed Christina, and the truth seemed to shift depending on who was speaking. Rumors fed the fire, including claims that Crawford tried to sabotage a Bette Davis project out of long-running animosity, further muddying the boundary between studio legend and reality. In the end, Mommie Dearest didn't settle the question of who Joan Crawford truly was; it ensured that the debate would never quite end.

470. David Carradine, an American actor best known for his role as Kwai Chang Caine in the 1970s television series *Kung Fu*, was found dead in a Bangkok hotel room in 2009. Authorities and an independent examiner

concluded the cause was accidental autoerotic asphyxiation. The circumstances were tragic, strange, and widely sensationalized.

471. Princess Isabella of Parma expressed deep emotion in her letters to her sister-in-law, revealing a strong personal bond and inner turmoil. She feared the repeated pregnancies expected of her as a royal consort, which took a toll on her physical and mental health. Weakened and despondent, she died of smallpox in 1763 at the age of 21. Her short life reflected the personal cost of royal expectations and duty.

472. R. Kelly faced decades of sexual abuse allegations. Accused of grooming young girls and running a "sex cult," he was convicted in 2021 of racketeering and sex trafficking. Once a celebrated R&B star, he is now serving a 30-year prison sentence.

473. In 2014, actor Michael Jace fatally shot his wife, April, in front of their 2 children. He was convicted of second-degree murder. The court sentenced him to 40 years to life in prison.

474. At age 23, actor Phill Lewis drove under the influence of alcohol in Maryland and caused a crash that killed 21-year-old Isabelle Duarte. He was convicted of vehicular manslaughter and DUI, receiving a 5-year sentence with most of it suspended. Lewis served a brief custodial term and completed over 300 hours of community service through a prison outreach program focused on the dangers of impaired driving. He later returned to television work and has since spoken publicly about the consequences of his actions.

475. Sean "Diddy" Combs has been accused by his partner, Cassie Ventura, and several others of abuse and coercive behavior. In 2024, surveillance footage emerged showing him assaulting Cassie in a hotel hallway in 2016. He publicly apologized for that incident but denied the wider allegations. He now faces multiple lawsuits and potential criminal investigations related to the claims.

476. Ezra Miller was filmed choking a woman in Iceland in 2020 and later arrested in Hawaii amid other allegations; they cited mental health treatment before *The Flash was* released to poor returns.

477. Michael Jackson lived in contradictions. He built Neverland Ranch as a childlike fantasy world filled with rides and animals, yet he also faced several allegations of child sexual abuse over the years. He was tried in court in 2005 and found not guilty on all charges, but the accusations stayed in the public conversation and changed the way many people viewed him.

478. Natalie Wood's mother was extremely controlling and allegedly encouraged her daughter to sleep with directors to get roles. At just 16, Wood was cast in "Rebel Without a Cause" after reportedly being told to sleep with the 42-year-old director. Her mother's influence left her vulnerable to exploitation throughout her career.

479. Indy 500 champion Jim Rathmann was born Royal Richard Rathmann — but as a teenager, he swapped names with his older brother so he could race underage. The switch stuck. He kept "Jim" for the rest of his life, and in 1960, he won the Indianapolis 500 under that adopted name. His greatest victory came with an alias on the trophy.

480. Queen Nzinga of Ndongo and Matamba defied gender roles with ferocity. She dressed in male clothing, kept a harem of cross-dressed men, and chose lovers through gladiator-style combat — executing the winner at dawn. In her later years, she married a female attendant, solidifying her legend as a ruler who obeyed no one's rules.

481. Whitney Houston's struggles were painfully public. She acknowledged in interviews that cocaine was a major part of her life during her marriage to Bobby Brown and long before it. Despite her incredible voice, addiction took a serious toll on her career and well-being. When she died in 2012, cocaine use and heart disease were listed as contributing factors.

482. Actress Tippi Hedren once stated that director Alfred Hitchcock subjected her to sexual harassment during their work together. She described a particularly traumatic incident involving real birds used during a violent scene in *The Birds*, which she believed was intended as punishment. After she rejected his advances, Hitchcock allegedly blocked her from accepting other roles while keeping her bound by contract.

483. Thandiwe Newton walked away from a role in *Charlie's Angels* after being asked to portray degrading and racist stereotypes. A director made

a crude comment about her body, and a studio executive suggested her character should be hyper-sexualized to be believable. Newton, a Cambridge graduate, refused to play along with those offensive ideas.

484. Katharine Hepburn defied conventions in life and love, forming deep bonds with both men and women. Yet she hated sex scenes and nudity, often walking off films that pushed either. A college friend once recalled she tried intercourse just once — and didn't care for it.

485. After watching a car plunge into Daytona's infield lake, rookie driver Tom Pistone took no chances. He qualified for his next race wearing a life preserver and an oxygen tube.

486. Jesse James, then married to Sandra Bullock, was exposed in 2010 when multiple women came forward claiming affairs. The revelations shattered their marriage shortly after Bullock won her Oscar, and the scandal made James one of Hollywood's most notorious cheaters.

487. In 1987, actor Matthew Broderick was involved in a fatal car accident while driving a rental vehicle in Northern Ireland. He mistakenly drove on the American side of the road, causing a head-on collision that killed Margaret Doherty and Anna Gallagher. Initially charged with dangerous driving, the charge was later reduced to careless driving, for which he received a fine of approximately $175.

488. Gian Gastone de' Medici, the last ruling Medici Grand Duke of Tuscany, reigned from 1723 until his death in 1737. He spent much of this period in seclusion, often confined to his bed and surrounded by companions. He withdrew from public duties and was known for his declining health and personal excesses, sometimes becoming physically ill during official functions. Despite his reclusive lifestyle, Florence's silk industry experienced significant growth during his rule, marking an unexpected period of economic success.

489. Britney Spears' 2007 breakdown became tabloid fodder. After shaving her head and confronting paparazzi with an umbrella, she was placed under a court-ordered conservatorship. The case later sparked worldwide discussions about personal autonomy and exploitation in the entertainment industry.

490. The so-called "chicken incident" at an Alice Cooper concert became one of rock's most notorious moments. During a 1969 show, Cooper threw a live chicken into the crowd, mistakenly believing it could fly. Instead, the bird was attacked and killed by the audience. Though unintentional, the incident fueled Cooper's shock-rock reputation and became a lasting part of music history.

491. Dennis Rodman became known for his eccentric and highly public persona both on and off the basketball court. He once staged a publicity event where he wore a bridal gown and claimed to marry himself, had a brief relationship with Madonna, frequently changed his hair color, and even participated in professional wrestling alongside Hulk Hogan. He later formed an unexpected friendship with North Korean leader Kim Jong-un. At one point during his NBA career, he also faced controversy for kicking a courtside cameraman.

492. Queen Elizabeth II had a staffer wear new shoes to avoid blisters and preferred her sandwiches crustless and without corners. The oddly specific snack mirrored old superstitions that linked sharp corners to coffin shapes. Even the most modern monarchs carried echoes of older fears.

493. Mel Gibson's career suffered after a series of public scandals. In 2006, he was arrested for driving under the influence and made an anti-Semitic remark to police officers. Later, recordings surfaced of him using racist and abusive language toward his former partner, which damaged his reputation and affected his career for years.

494. In 2017, long-standing allegations against film producer Harvey Weinstein came to light, revealing decades of sexual harassment and assault that had been widely rumored within the film industry. He was convicted in multiple U.S. trials and sentenced to lengthy prison terms, though one conviction was later overturned. Weinstein remains incarcerated on separate charges, and his case became a major catalyst for the global #MeToo movement.

495. Queen Mary, grandmother to Elizabeth II, had a well-known habit of "collecting" from her hosts. She'd admire an object in silence until the owner offered it — or watched it vanish mysteriously. Palace aides quietly

returned the items later, often with a polite note citing a "misunderstanding."

496. At Versailles, Marie Antoinette, the last queen of France before the French Revolution, commissioned the construction of a mock peasant village known as the Hameau de la Reine, where she could retreat from court life. The estate included working dairies, gardens, and servants dressed in costume, while the queen herself wore fine fabrics and used ornate props to play at simplicity. Intended as a private escape, the display only deepened public resentment, reinforcing perceptions of royal detachment. It did little to shield her from the political unrest that ultimately led to her execution.

497. John Quincy Adams made a habit of skinny-dipping at dawn in the Potomac River. Journalist Anne Royall allegedly hid his clothes one morning to force an interview. He wasn't the only president to swim nude — but he may have been the most extorted.

498. Dolley Madison's famous "Wednesday squeezes" packed the White House with everyone from cobblers to congressmen. She wore bold colors, laughed loudly, and made politics feel like a party. In a stiff young capital, Dolley brought charisma and champagne.

499. At a private royal party in Thailand, Princess Srirasmi became the center of a notorious leaked video: nearly nude, laughing as she poured drinks for guests while the palace poodle, Fufu, trotted through the room like a dignitary. The absurdity wasn't just for show — Fufu had been ceremonially named an air chief marshal, complete with public appearances and, later, a four-day funeral that drew headlines for its pageantry.

Behind the spectacle lay turbulence. The episode fed gossip about the monarchy's inner circle just as palace factions were shifting. In the years that followed, Srirasmi's world collapsed: scandal, scrutiny, and a steep fall from favor. What looked like a surreal party trick now reads as a prelude to deeper palace drama.

500. Betty Ford broke every First Lady mold. She campaigned over CB radio as "Big Mama," wore a mood ring, danced at state events, and spoke openly about premarital sex, marijuana, and her own addiction. Her honesty reshaped how the country saw treatment — and itself.

501. Lady Bird Johnson underwent a premarital exam after a whirlwind honeymoon, worried about her new husband's intense libido. Later, she even mimicked the look of one of Lyndon's mistresses, trying to keep his wandering attention. She knew that divorce would destroy his political future — and hers.

502. Marie Curie uniquely won Nobel Prizes in 2 different sciences: the Nobel Prize in Physics in 1903 for her pioneering research on radiation, and the Nobel Prize in Chemistry in 1911 for her discovery of the elements polonium and radium. She was the first female laureate and remains singular for dual scientific Nobels across disciplines.

503. Jack White has a taste for the macabre and the obscure. He collects taxidermy — including a mounted elephant head he once bought on live TV — and owns artifacts like Al Capone's prison compositions and mental asylum scrapbooks. He also has a deep dislike of nurses.

504. Peter Sellers was notoriously volatile on set — he'd lash out at crew, demand firings, and use chaos to keep control. He also developed intense superstitions, treating the color purple as an omen of death. If he saw it on set or in a hotel room, he'd erupt or walk out entirely.

505. Multiple male massage therapists and a cruise worker accused John Travolta of sexual misconduct; the cases were denied by his lawyer, and some were withdrawn or steered to private resolution.

506. Robert Downey Jr. nearly lost everything to addiction. In the 1990s, he was arrested several times for heroin and cocaine possession, and on one occasion, wandered into a neighbor's home while under the influence. His remarkable comeback as Iron Man became one of Hollywood's most celebrated turnarounds.

507. ZZ Top's bass player, Dusty Hill, once took a break from fame by working incognito at an airport, just to "stay grounded." Years earlier, he toured the U.S. as part of a fake "Zombies" band before finding his way back to the blues. Eventually, he reclaimed the beard, the bass, and the spotlight.

508. In 2021, actor Armie Hammer faced public fallout after multiple women shared disturbing messages and alleged violent sexual fantasies.

Though an LAPD investigation closed without charges, he lost major film roles and agency representation. His career remains in limbo.

509. Tiger Woods' image collapsed in 2009. Following a car accident outside his home, multiple women came forward alleging extramarital affairs. The scandal cost him major sponsorships, led to a widely publicized apology, and significantly altered the trajectory of his career.

510. NASCAR driver Dale Earnhardt Jr. keeps a personal junkyard called "Dirty Mo Acres" filled with wrecked race cars — including one stuck in a tree. He's also been known to use his own discarded chassis for target practice. It's a scrapyard-meets-shooting range for speed demons.

511. Tom DeLonge turned from pop-punk to a full-blown paranormal investigator. He founded a UFO research network, claims government surveillance, helped popularize Navy UFO videos — and now searches for Bigfoot.

512. Orson Welles was self-conscious about the size of his nose and wore custom-made prosthetic noses in nearly all of his film appearances. He was known to keep a collection of them, some of which he named, and would occasionally use them in party tricks and magic performances. The prosthetics became a personal trademark both on and off screen.

513. Calvin Coolidge believed in quiet routines — and strange ones. Each morning in bed, he had petroleum jelly massaged into his scalp, thinking it promoted health. It was an era when pharmacies casually sold cocaine-laced tonics and radium water.

514. In 1969, Jimmy Carter reported seeing a bright, color-shifting object in the sky and later filed a formal UFO report. He even campaigned on government transparency about extraterrestrial phenomena. But once in office, he backed away, citing national security concerns.

515. Stephen Morris, drummer for Joy Division and New Order, relaxes by driving retired military tanks. He's even staged mock battles using postal vans as enemy targets. He admits the experience is fun, but the interiors are less than glamorous.

516. In 1969, Senator Ted Kennedy drove off the Dike Bridge on Chappaquiddick Island, resulting in the death of passenger Mary Jo Kopechne,

who was trapped in the submerged car. Kennedy escaped but didn't report the incident to authorities until the following morning. He later pleaded guilty to leaving the scene of an accident and received a suspended 2-month sentence. Though he remained a prominent figure in the U.S. Senate, the incident significantly damaged his national political prospects.

517. Winona Ryder's shoplifting arrest in 2001 shocked fans. She was caught taking designer clothing and accessories valued at over $5,000 from Saks Fifth Avenue. The incident resulted in probation, community service, and fines, damaging her reputation, though she later rebuilt her career and returned to the spotlight.

518. As a teenager, future NASCAR driver Dale Jarrett tried to replace mowing the lawn with 2 goats. They ignored the grass and instead chewed through car interiors — tearing vinyl roofs and seat upholstery. The plan ended quickly, with a barely trimmed yard and damaged furniture.

519. Johnny Depp and Amber Heard each accused the other of serious abuse during their legal disputes. Depp lost a 2020 libel case in the U.K., but in a separate 2022 defamation trial in the U.S., a Virginia jury largely ruled in his favor while also awarding Heard a partial victory on one of her counterclaims.

520. In 1988, actor Rob Lowe recorded a sexual encounter with 2 women he met at a nightclub, later discovering that one was 16 years old. No criminal charges were filed after a legal agreement was reached. Lowe has since stated that the scandal was a turning point in his life and played a role in his decision to pursue sobriety.

521. Nancy Spungen was found stabbed to death in 1978 at New York's Chelsea Hotel, where she had been staying with her boyfriend, Sid Vicious of the rock band Sex Pistols. Vicious initially confessed but later claimed he had no memory of the event, saying he had been asleep. Both had been using heroin heavily, and after a suicide attempt and time in jail, Vicious was released on bail. He died of an overdose before standing trial, leaving the circumstances of Spungen's death officially unresolved.

522. In the late 19th century, Prussian Princess Charlotte threw lavish, scandalous orgies for the aristocracy, then used letters and sketches to

blackmail her guests. A duel and an arrest followed, but she escaped untouched. Her parties were both a trap and a spectacle.

523. Aerosmith's Steven Tyler claims he spent at least $5 to $6 million on cocaine over his lifetime.

524. In 2015, Charlie Sheen publicly revealed that he was HIV-positive. Following his disclosure, some former partners claimed he had not informed them beforehand. Sheen acknowledged paying settlements to keep the diagnosis private but stated that he had not transmitted the virus to anyone.

525. Cary Grant credited LSD with changing his life and publicly urged others to try it after more than 100 guided sessions between 1958 and 1961. He gave startling descriptions of visions and said it "released inhibition."

526. Marilyn Monroe's glamour masked deep pain. She struggled with depression, depended on prescription barbiturates, and had high-profile relationships, including with President John F. Kennedy. Her sudden death in 1962, officially ruled a probable suicide, remains one of Hollywood's most enduring mysteries.

527. At the 1913 Indy 500, French driver Jules Goux drank between 4 and 6 bottles of champagne during the race. He made his pit crew top him off at stops and still won by 13 minutes. After that, race-day alcohol was banned for good.

10. Absurd Laws & Political Blunders

Government and legislation can be unintentionally ridiculous. Mistyped laws, strange bans, and odd traditions reveal that even serious institutions sometimes stumble into absurdity.

528. In its effort to compete with Airbus, Boeing accelerated development of the 737 MAX, incorporating a flight control system called MCAS. Inadequate disclosure and training around the system contributed to 2 fatal crashes in 2018 and 2019, which killed everyone on board. The incidents led to a global grounding of the fleet and caused significant financial losses and reputational harm for Boeing. The aircraft was only cleared to return to service after extensive review and design changes.

529. After a shaky debate performance in 2024, Joe Biden lost a lot of support from his own party, eventually stepping out of the race and throwing his weight behind Kamala Harris. But in the end, Donald Trump and J.D. Vance scored a big win, making Trump only the second U.S. president ever to serve non-consecutive terms.

530. Dueling is a thing of the past and has no place in today's military. Attempting to challenge someone to a fight, especially with weapons, is not only inappropriate — it can lead to disciplinary action for endangering yourself and others. Modern military protocol resolves conflicts through formal channels, such as counseling and command intervention, not personal combat.

531. In 2022, Liz Truss became the shortest-serving prime minister in British history, resigning after just 49 days in office. Her downfall stemmed from a "mini-budget" packed with unfunded tax cuts and heavy borrowing, a gamble meant to boost growth but one that sent markets into freefall. The pound crashed to record lows, borrowing costs surged, and the Bank of England was forced to step in to stabilize the economy.

The chaos eroded Truss's authority almost immediately, sparking a political meltdown inside her own party. By October, she announced her resignation, her brief tenure cemented as a cautionary tale of economic overreach and political miscalculation.

532. In China's Xinjiang region, authorities implemented mass detention, coercive labor transfers, intrusive surveillance, and family-separation policies targeting Uyghurs and other Muslim minorities; multiple governments and bodies have labeled the abuses crimes against humanity or genocide, which Beijing denies.

533. In 1978, British Prime Minister James Callaghan, leading the Labour government, chose not to call a general election despite favorable polling, expecting better conditions the following year. However, the "Winter of Discontent," a wave of strikes over pay and inflation that lasted from 1978 to 1979, badly damaged Labour's reputation and contributed to Margaret Thatcher's Conservative victory in the 1979 election.

534. In 2009, Prime Minister Gordon Brown decided not to hold a referendum on the Lisbon Treaty, a move that many critics say deepened public mistrust of Westminster and helped set the stage for Brexit. The treaty reorganized the workings of the European Union and shifted some powers to Brussels. Although the Labour government had hinted at a public vote, Brown declined. For Eurosceptics, this became proof that ordinary voters were being excluded from major decisions about Europe.

That choice, while less famous than David Cameron's later Brexit referendum, is now seen as an early spark in Britain's tensions with the European Union. It highlighted a growing divide between politicians and voters, a theme that would dominate U.K. politics for the next decade and pave the way for the historic Brexit vote in 2016.

535. Georgia requires fried chicken to be eaten with your hands. Using utensils isn't allowed, even if food is messy or covered in sauce. Though intended humorously, this ordinance technically remains law, emphasizing Georgia's cultural connection to fried chicken and Southern traditions in a quirky way.

536. Jumping off a military ship for a quick swim is a fast way to sink your career. Whether in port, at anchor, or at sea, going overboard without authorization is dangerous and punishable. Outcomes can include loss of pay, confinement, or a trip out of the service.

537. In Arcadia, Greece, peacocks have the right of way. If one crosses the road, drivers are legally required to wait, no matter how long it takes.

538. Massachusetts has a quirky, rarely enforced law stating it's unlawful to sleep without bathing first.

539. U.S. national security officials — including the vice president, defense secretary, and top intelligence chiefs — were secretly planning military strikes on the Houthis in Yemen via a Signal group chat. But thanks to a bizarre iPhone mishap, *The Atlantic's* editor Jeffrey Goldberg was accidentally added to the conversation — where war plans, strike timings, and even a CIA operative's name were laid out in real time.

Goldberg published the transcripts, and the situation quickly exploded into "Signalgate" — a full-blown scandal that left Trump officials scrambling, sparked outrage over lax security, and led to congressional hearings.

540. During a 2000 visit to Israel's Yad Vashem memorial, German Chancellor Gerhard Schröder accidentally extinguished the eternal flame by turning the control the wrong way. Aides had to relight it with a gas lighter as cameras captured the moment. Given the solemn setting and historical context, the symbolism of the mishap was deeply amplified.

541. In the military, faking illness is known as malingering, and it's treated as a serious offense. Service members who pretend to be sick can face significant disciplinary action, while those who intentionally harm themselves to avoid duty may face even harsher punishment — especially in a combat zone. It's not seen as a shortcut but as a severe breach of duty.

542. Poland banned Winnie the Pooh from public spaces, citing concerns over the character's lack of pants and ambiguous gender. People have reportedly been fined for wearing Pooh-themed shirts, making it one of Europe's strangest examples of censorship in pop culture.

543. Canadian radio stations are legally required to play at least 35% Canadian music. By doing this, they ensure Canadian artists receive exposure, though many listeners now use streaming platforms like Spotify or Apple Music, where such national content quotas don't apply, and music selection is unrestricted.

544. In Singapore, chewing gum is banned except for medical purposes. Selling gum can result in fines of up to $100,000 or 2 years in prison, and

failing to flush a public toilet carries a $150 fine. Both laws aim to maintain strict cleanliness standards.

545. William Henry Harrison gave the longest U.S. inaugural address — outside, coatless, in freezing weather. He soon developed pneumonia, was treated with 1840s "cures" like bloodletting, and died a month later. The record-length speech produced the shortest presidency.

546. In Alabama, wearing a fake mustache that causes laughter in church is illegal. Other odd American laws include Iowa banning kisses longer than 5 minutes and South Dakota banning intimacy if underwear smells like garlic.

547. In Toronto and Ottawa, Canada, climbing trees in public spaces is banned. A man fined $365 in 2013 for climbing a tree sparked controversy, but the law remains in effect to prevent injuries and damage to protected urban trees in heavily visited parks.

548. Beginning in 2016 and intensifying in 2017, Myanmar's military launched a violent campaign against the Rohingya minority, resulting in the destruction of villages and the mass displacement of over 700,000 people to refugee camps in Bangladesh. A United Nations fact-finding mission later concluded there was credible evidence of genocidal intent. International efforts to pursue accountability are ongoing through legal and human rights channels.

549. Florida has a rule banning farting in public after 6:00 p.m. on Thursdays. Like many humorous ordinances, it's a relic of local codes that were never repealed. Its sheer absurdity makes it one of Florida's most frequently cited "weird laws."

550. Mumbai once imposed a ban on dancing in bars, aiming to reduce crime and exploitation. While the law was intended to protect women from trafficking and abuse, it led to the closure of thousands of establishments and sparked controversy. Critics argued it unfairly targeted performers and undermined cultural expression and livelihoods.

551. In 1588, King Philip II of Spain, who reigned from 1580 to 1598, launched the Spanish Armada, a massive fleet meant to invade England and overthrow Queen Elizabeth I. Command was given to the Duke of

Medina Sidonia, a nobleman with little naval experience, setting the stage for disaster. Though Spain's ships were formidable, poor coordination, logistical failures, and outbreaks of disease weakened the fleet. English forces, using faster, more maneuverable ships and daring tactics, inflicted heavy damage.

Nature finished what England started: brutal storms scattered the Armada as it retreated north, sinking ships along Ireland's coasts. The defeat shattered Spain's aura of naval invincibility and marked a turning point in global power. England's maritime rise began, while Spain's dominance faded for generations. The Armada's failure became a cautionary tale of overconfidence and hubris — proof that even the mightiest empire could be humbled by strategy, weather, and fate.

552. In 1804, Napoleon ordered the kidnapping and execution of the Duc d'Enghien, a Bourbon prince accused of plotting against him. The act outraged Europe's aristocracy and alienated powerful figures, including the Russian Tsar, undermining Napoleon's diplomatic standing. It inspired the famous remark attributed to Talleyrand, Fouché, or the Comte de la Meurthe: "It was worse than a crime; it was a mistake!"

553. In 2016, Dennis Hastert, the longest-serving Republican Speaker of the U.S. House of Representatives, was convicted of financial crimes related to hush money payments made to cover up his sexual abuse of boys during his time as a high school wrestling coach. Because the abuse itself was beyond the statute of limitations, he was only sentenced to 15 months in prison, serving 13.

554. Japan's surrender negotiations in 1945 were derailed when U.S. officials interpreted "mokusatsu," meaning "no comment," as rejection. Believing Japan defiant, the U.S. dropped atomic bombs on Hiroshima and Nagasaki, killing over 100,000 people. Truman never apologized, and nuclear weapons became a grim symbol of ultimate deterrence.

555. Running out of gas on Germany's Autobahn is illegal. Drivers must ensure vehicles are road-ready, and stopping unnecessarily on high-speed highways can result in fines of up to $70. The rule emphasizes safety, as breakdowns on the Autobahn are extremely dangerous.

556. In parts of Spain, building sandcastles or elaborate sand sculptures on beaches is banned, with fines in place for those who break the rule. These restrictions, often tied to safety concerns and environmental preservation, aim to keep crowded tourist beaches safe and accessible, though they've drawn criticism for being overly strict.

557. In India, kite-flying technically requires a government license, with fines for unlicensed flying reaching 500 rupees (around $5). The law dates back to aviation regulations aimed at preventing injuries from dangerous string coated with glass or metal, but today it's rarely enforced and stands out as one of India's quirkiest aviation rules.

558. Portugal makes it illegal to urinate in the ocean, though enforcement is nearly impossible. The law was designed to protect beaches and water quality, but has become a frequent target of ridicule due to the practical challenges of catching violators mid-violation.

559. Milan, Italy, once required residents to smile at all times, except during funerals or hospital visits. Though not enforced today, it reflects Italy's historical emphasis on positivity and politeness, even if its practicality in daily life made it a law that faded over time.

560. New Jersey once had a quirky law prohibiting the purchase of ice cream after 6:00 p.m. without a doctor's note. Though it's no longer enforced, this odd regulation lingers in state legal codes.

561. Taking selfies with Buddha statues is illegal in Sri Lanka because turning your back to Buddha is considered disrespectful. A British tourist was jailed for 3 days in 2014 for breaking this rule, demonstrating Sri Lanka's strict enforcement of religious respect.

562. Canada bans bringing llamas into its national parks, a rule designed to protect native wildlife and preserve fragile ecosystems. While few travelers own pet llamas, the regulation helps prevent disease transmission and disruption caused by non-native animals, reflecting the strict conservation policies of Parks Canada.

563. During the Ming Dynasty, China halted its large-scale maritime expeditions and shifted toward isolation. Long-distance trade was limited, and Confucian officials emphasized self-sufficiency over external

commerce. While this inward turn addressed short-term security and political concerns, it caused China to fall behind other nations in navigation, technology, and global diplomacy. The empire remained powerful, but its influence on the world stage gradually diminished.

564. In Virginia, hunting on Sundays is banned unless targeting raccoons. Raccoons were likely considered agricultural pests, leading lawmakers to create this odd exception. Historically, hunting restrictions on Sundays came from "blue laws" designed to enforce rest and religious observance across communities.

565. In Virginia, an old statute makes it illegal to tickle women, reflecting outdated laws meant to govern personal conduct.

566. In 2010, Ed Miliband narrowly defeated his brother David Miliband to become leader of the U.K. Labour Party — a result political commentator David Fuller called "hugely consequential." The leadership upset influenced Labour's stance on military intervention in Syria and ushered in leadership rule changes that later paved the way for Jeremy Corbyn's rise.

567. Keeping hands in pockets was once strictly prohibited across all military branches. While some have relaxed the rule in casual settings, it still applies in formation, while on duty, or whenever it affects military bearing. In uniform, comfort takes a back seat to readiness and professional appearance.

568. Senator William Seward, long viewed as the likely Republican nominee for president, weakened his candidacy by taking a 9-month European tour and becoming entangled in abolitionist controversy. Delegates switched to Abraham Lincoln, who won the nomination, led the Union to victory, and reshaped the nation permanently.

569. Ulysses S. Grant failed to fully protect Black voters as white supremacist violence surged. In 1876, Rutherford B. Hayes secured the presidency by agreeing to withdraw federal troops, effectively ending Reconstruction. Black Southerners were left defenseless as Jim Crow took hold.

570. President Richard Nixon approved the Watergate break-in and directed the cover-up, even though he was likely to win reelection without it. The scandal eventually forced his resignation and deeply damaged public trust in government. When Gerald Ford later pardoned Nixon, the decision was intended to help the country move forward — but for many, it reinforced the perception that those in power could escape accountability.

571. Cheating isn't just a bad look in a military uniform — it can be a crime. If an affair harms good order or embarrasses the service, commanders can punish it with rank cuts, pay loss, confinement, or even a discharge. In military law, it's "extramarital sexual conduct," and it can end careers fast.

572. Signed in 1919, the Treaty of Versailles was meant to secure peace after World War 1, but instead planted the seeds of another global conflict. Germany was forced to accept full blame for the war, pay $33 billion in reparations (about $582 billion today), surrender territory, and drastically reduce its military. The treaty humiliated Germany and shattered its economy, leading to mass unemployment, runaway inflation, and deep national resentment.

This climate of despair and anger became fertile ground for extremism. Adolf Hitler and the Nazi Party exploited the outrage, portraying the treaty as a betrayal and using promises of revenge and restoration to gain power. Within 2 decades, Europe was plunged into World War 2, making Versailles not a symbol of peace but a cautionary tale of how punishing terms can destabilize nations and ignite future wars.

573. King Charles I bypassed Parliament, levied "ship money" annually, and imprisoned dissenters, ruling alone for 11 years. His disregard for governance traditions fueled unrest, sparked the English Civil Wars, and ultimately led to his 1649 execution, temporarily abolishing the monarchy and turning England into a short-lived republic.

574. In 2019, Hunter Biden's abandoned laptop revealed emails linking him and Joe Biden to foreign business dealings. Social media companies suppressed the story, allegedly influenced by the FBI, sparking accusations of censorship, election interference, and shielding the Biden family.

575. In Samoa, forgetting your wife's birthday is a crime. Husbands receive warnings for a first offense, but repeat offenders can face jail time. The law reflects Samoa's cultural emphasis on marital respect, though its enforcement is mostly symbolic and rarely results in arrests.

576. Argentina forbids naming children after famous or fictional figures, including Lionel Messi. The restriction is meant to maintain cultural identity and prevent overuse of certain names, though it frustrates fans who wish to name their children after sports or pop culture icons.

577. In Oregon, fortune-telling and similar occult practices are banned, including crystal ball readings, tarot cards, or anything resembling psychic services, which lawmakers likely considered scams. Fortune-telling is regulated or banned in several states, though many view such laws as outdated restrictions on harmless entertainment.

578. In Bermuda, it's technically illegal to walk barefoot in public without a permit, a law rooted in old public decency standards.

579. Candles start over 15,000 house fires each year in the U.S., making up about 4% of all residential fires. This surprising statistic shows how a simple household item can pose serious danger if left unattended.

580. Florida bans singing in public while wearing a swimsuit. Anyone belting out tunes at a beach or pool could technically violate this rule, though modern social norms make such laws feel obsolete and unnecessary today.

581. The 2020 Doha Agreement, negotiated under President Trump, set a fixed date for U.S. withdrawal from Afghanistan, excluded the Afghan government from direct talks, and required the release of Taliban prisoners without securing a lasting peace. When President Biden carried out the withdrawal in 2021, the process was marred by intelligence failures and limited contingency planning. The result was a rapid Taliban advance and a chaotic evacuation from Kabul.

582. In 2022, the U.S. Supreme Court's decision in Dobbs v. Jackson Women's Health Organization overturned Roe v. Wade, removing the federal constitutional right to abortion. As a result, access to abortion now varies by state, with some enacting near-total bans and others strength-

ening legal protections. The ruling has led to increased interstate travel for reproductive healthcare and ongoing legal and political disputes across the country.

583. In 2023, Canada's Parliament gave a standing ovation to 98-year-old Yaroslav Hunka during Ukrainian President Volodymyr Zelensky's visit, unaware he had served in a Waffen-SS Nazi unit during World War 2. The incident sparked outrage, with Jewish organizations demanding transparency over wartime immigration records. House Speaker Anthony Rota resigned, and Prime Minister Justin Trudeau issued formal apologies to Zelensky, Jewish communities, and Canadians.

584. Maine makes it illegal to bite your landlord. While biting anyone is already assault, this law calls out landlords specifically, likely after an incident where a tenant bit their property manager.

585. In some French beaches, men are only allowed to wear Speedos, banning board shorts or other swimwear. The regulation emphasizes hygiene and tradition but feels intrusive and embarrassing to many tourists, adding a strange twist to beach fashion rules in certain regions.

586. In 1971, President Richard Nixon had a secret taping system installed in the Oval Office and other key White House rooms to record conversations automatically. Intended as a tool for accuracy and record-keeping, the tapes later became pivotal evidence in the Watergate scandal, ultimately leading to Nixon's resignation.

11. Dark Laughs & Bizarre Headlines

News can be stranger than fiction. From high-flying emergencies and citywide riots to reporters facing danger live on air, reality delivers chaos, comedy, and shock in equal measure.

587. A JetBlue flight had malfunctioning landing gear in 2005, forcing the plane to circle and burn fuel before safely landing in Los Angeles. Passengers watched the emergency unfold live on in-flight TV.

588. A massive blue light lit up the New York City sky in 2018, causing panic among residents. It turned out to be a transformer explosion in Astoria that created an electrical arc visible for miles.

589. In June 2011, Vancouver, Canada, erupted in chaos after the hometown Canucks lost Game 7 of the Stanley Cup Finals to the Boston Bruins. What began as disappointment quickly spiraled into one of the country's worst sports riots. Thousands of fans crowded downtown streets, overturning cars, smashing windows, and looting stores as fires broke out across the city.

The destruction was staggering: nearly $10 million in damages, hundreds of arrests, and at least 15 serious injuries, including stabbings. Images of burning vehicles and bloodied fans shocked a nation known for its calm reputation, prompting comparisons to a similar riot after the Canucks' 1994 Stanley Cup loss.

In the aftermath, Vancouver residents rallied to clean up their city, covering boarded-up shop windows with notes of apology and encouragement. The event became a sobering reminder of how quickly passion for sports can turn violent, leaving scars that take years to heal.

590. A news helicopter lost control and crashed onto a Brooklyn rooftop in 2004. Despite the dramatic footage, everyone aboard survived with only minor injuries.

591. While covering a water main break in West Virginia, reporter Tori Yorgi was struck by a car during a live broadcast. Remarkably, she stood

up immediately, laughed off the incident, and reassured viewers she was okay — earning praise for her resilience and professionalism.

592. Indian news anchor Supreet Kaur remained composed while reporting a fatal road accident — suspecting, but not confirming, that her husband was among the dead. Only after signing off did she confirm the worst and break down off-camera. Her professionalism stunned viewers and colleagues alike.

593. During a 2011 tornado outbreak, a WREX meteorologist evacuated the newsroom while on air and continued broadcasting from the basement as the tornado neared.

594. In 2011, Lauren Giddings, a recent graduate of Mercer Law School, was reported missing in Macon, Georgia. Her neighbor, Steven McDaniel, gave a television interview in which he appeared to react in real time to the discovery of a dismembered torso — later identified as Giddings. Investigators found evidence linking McDaniel to the crime, including a master key to her apartment, voyeuristic digital files, and a saw with traces of her blood. He eventually confessed to the murder and is currently serving a life sentence in prison.

595. In September 2016, during a live taping of *Sports Final* at WBZ-TV in Boston, sportscaster Steve Burton lost control of a taped baby alligator, causing a brief panic before handlers calmed the situation.

596. In 1994, CBS aired *Without Warning*, a fictional special that interrupted regular programming with a fake newscast reporting asteroid impacts in Wyoming, France, and China. Real news anchors and correspondents played themselves, lending the broadcast a sense of authenticity, while dramatic cutaways depicted craters, military lockdowns, and a Search for Extraterrestrial Intelligence scientist warning of possible extraterrestrial contact. Although CBS displayed on-screen disclaimers and repeated them during commercial breaks — with some affiliates adding additional crawl text — many viewers still called stations to ask if the events were real. The program ended with a chilling twist: screens filled with incoming objects, the studio lost power, and the anchor closed with a quote from Shakespeare. The special underscored how realistic

presentation and familiar news formats can temporarily override skepticism, even when disclaimers are present.

597. Franco Scoglio, a legendary Italian football coach and TV pundit, collapsed mid-sentence during a live debate about Genoa CFC. The station quickly cut away and called emergency services, but he couldn't be revived. He died doing what he loved — arguing about football on air.

598. In 2016, a KTVU reporter narrowly escaped being hit by a car during a live broadcast when a quick-thinking photographer shouted a warning. The vehicle ended up striking the camera instead, capturing the dramatic near-miss on tape.

599. The bullfighting festival of July 9, 2016, turned tragic when Lorenzo — a 1,166-pound bull (or 529 kilograms) — fatally gored Spanish matador Víctor Barrio, a moment broadcast live. Despite immediate treatment, he was pronounced dead at the hospital, the first such case in Spain in over 3 decades.

600. In 2007, a televised sting by Dateline NBC's *To Catch a Predator* took a tragic turn when officers attempted to arrest Texas prosecutor Louis Conradt after hours of failed contact. As cameras rolled nearby, Conradt died by suicide inside his home. The incident sparked intense backlash, raising questions about the show's collaboration with law enforcement, the validity of warrants, and the ethics of made-for-TV justice. In the aftermath, multiple prosecutions fell apart, and the show was effectively canceled.

601. In December 1986, near San Diego, 20-year-old Cara Knott was found strangled beneath a highway bridge. Days later, a local TV station aired a roadside safety PSA featuring California Highway Patrol officer Craig Alan Peyer, who advised drivers to stay inside their vehicles when pulled over. After the segment aired, multiple women came forward with reports of coercive late-night stops by Peyer along that same highway stretch. Investigators found rope in his trunk, and fabric under Knott's nails matched material from police uniforms. Peyer was arrested 2 weeks after the broadcast and later convicted of her murder.

602. Cabbages & Condoms is a condom-themed restaurant chain in Bangkok where guests receive a condom instead of a mint.

603. In 1985, a fire broke out at Bradford City's Valley Parade stadium when a cigarette ember ignited accumulated rubbish beneath aging wooden seating. Within minutes, the stand was engulfed in flames, killing 56 people and injuring 265. The tragedy led to major reforms in stadium fire safety in the U.K., including bans on smoking near wooden structures and stricter building regulations for sports venues.

604. On Queen's Day in Apeldoorn, April 30, 2009, a driver purposefully cut through the crowd and crashed beside the royal family's open-top bus. As audiences watched live, 7 people were killed, and several were injured. The driver later died, and authorities identified the attack as directed at the royals.

605. In 2012, Mick Philpott set his Derby house on fire to frame an ex and stage a rescue; the blaze killed 6 of his children. Covert recordings and forensics led to his conviction alongside accomplices.

606. In 2015, reporter Alison Parker and cameraman Adam Ward were tragically shot and killed during a live interview in Virginia by a disgruntled former colleague. The interviewee, though injured in the attack, survived the ordeal, which shocked viewers and sparked national conversations about workplace violence and media safety.

607. In 1984, on ITV's *Live from Her Majesty's*, comedian Tommy Cooper collapsed mid-act while the audience laughed, thinking it was shtick. The curtain dropped, the show cut to commercials, and he was pronounced dead shortly after.

608. In 2012, the Peruvian television show *El valor de la verdad* premiered with 19-year-old Ruth Thalía Sayas as its first guest. During the polygraph-based program, she revealed in front of her family and boyfriend that she had worked as a stripper and engaged in sex work. Weeks later, her ex-boyfriend, Bryan Romero, murdered her. He was later convicted and sentenced to life in prison.

609. On Italy's TG2 news program, fathers' rights activist Nicola De Martino stunned viewers by dousing himself in lighter fluid live on air. He was stopped before striking a match, then briefly allowed to paraphrase a statement before the host swiftly cut the broadcast. The moment became a grim flashpoint in Italy's family law debates.

610. On June 25, 2007, WWE aired a live tribute to wrestler Chris Benoit after news broke of the deaths of him and his family. The following day, authorities announced that Benoit had killed his wife and son before taking his own life. A later examination of his brain revealed extensive damage consistent with chronic traumatic encephalopathy. In response to the tragedy, WWE removed or significantly reduced Benoit's presence from its archives and public materials.

611. On August 19, 1987, Gary Stollman entered KNBC in Burbank during a live segment, pointed an unloaded BB gun at David Horowitz, and forced him to read a bizarre CIA involvement and alien clones. Stollman surrendered immediately, and no one was hurt.

612. During a severe storm in Chattanooga, Tennessee, WRCB meteorologist Paul Barys kept calmly issuing safety instructions as golf-ball-sized hail slammed the studio "like a jackhammer." Moments after he warned of escalation, a tornado warning was officially issued. His timing and poise gave viewers precious minutes to take cover.

613. During Japan's March 11, 2011, disaster — a magnitude 9.1 earthquake followed by a massive tsunami — live broadcasts on NHK captured the unfolding crisis in real time. As alarms sounded and the ground shook violently, news and weather presenters remained calm, delivering emergency guidance to the public. The disaster claimed approximately 15,900 lives and caused an estimated $360 billion in damage, making it one of the costliest natural disasters in history.

614. Buffalo firefighter Donald Herbert suffered a severe brain injury after a 1995 roof collapse left him without oxygen for 6 minutes. After nearly 10 years in a minimally conscious state, he astonishingly woke in 2005, spoke with family for hours, and recognized loved ones. Weeks later, he fell from bed during a violent episode, suffered a brain bleed, never regained lucidity, and died in 2006.

615. In 2014, Cards Against Humanity sold 30,000 boxes of literal bull feces on Black Friday.

616. During the 1999 *Over the Edge* pay-per-view event, professional wrestler Owen Hart died after a stunt entrance went tragically wrong. He fell approximately 78 feet (about 24 meters) from the rafters when his

harness malfunctioned, suffering fatal internal injuries. The broadcast briefly cut away, and although the accident wasn't shown on camera, the event continued, a decision that drew significant criticism. A settlement with Hart's family later contributed to the creation of the Owen Hart Foundation, supporting charitable causes in his memory.

617. During a live beach segment, a Fox reporter suddenly screamed and bolted off-camera when a giant flying insect swooped toward him. The unscripted moment aired live, delighting viewers and quickly going viral for the reporter's panicked reaction.

618. Brazilian priest Adelir Antônio de Carli used a cluster of helium balloons to raise money for a truckers' chapel. After a successful flight in January 2008, he attempted a second launch on April 20 using around 1,000 balloons. He didn't know how to operate his GPS and had no real-time knowledge of wind conditions. He flew into rain clouds, drifted out over the ocean at night, and eventually lost contact. Months later, only his lower body was recovered, suggesting he drowned after abandoning the flight. The stunt looked dramatic on television but lacked proper risk planning. De Carli placed his trust in faith and limited survival training but skipped practical GPS use and route coordination.

619. When 13-year-old Raisa disappeared while swimming in the Miriam River on June 29, 2025, a TV reporter stepped into the water to demonstrate concealed drop-offs and strong flow. He felt a "soft" object underfoot — what seemed like an arm — and locals immediately recovered her body from that precise location.

620. Virgin Boy Eggs are a controversial Chinese delicacy boiled in the urine of boys under 10.

621. In 2003, during a Mexican talk show segment with exotic animals, a young lion suddenly latched onto a toddler's pants and tried to bite. Handlers quickly stepped in, urging calm while prying the lion away. Miraculously, the child was unharmed — but the clip went viral as a chilling near miss.

622. In an ABC News segment, a man claiming he could summon UFOs invited the crew to witness the phenomenon at a specific time and location. As cameras rolled under a clear sky, several bright objects — most

notably an orange sphere — appeared, hovered in the distance, and then vanished. The unexpected display left the news team visibly stunned and sparked debate over whether it was a coincidence, misidentification, or something more mysterious.

623. A live segment on Japan's TV Miyazaki in 2008 had contestants shoving each other off a platform into shallow water and mud. Host Tetsuchi Yanagida dove headfirst, broke his neck, and was instantly paralyzed. Believing he was clowning, staff repeatedly pushed his face back into the mud before realizing he was drowning; he survived but remained paralyzed.

624. On April 28, 2014, as sirens howled over Tupelo, Mississippi, meteorologist Matt Laubhan watched a multi-vortex tornado hook toward the city — and toward his own station. The lights flickered, the radar filled with red, and he cut through the tension with a clear command: staff to shelter, now. Then he stayed put. While colleagues moved off the floor, Laubhan kept broadcasting, voice steady over the roar of the storm, repeating street-level warnings and telling viewers exactly when to get underground.

It was a rare moment when television became a lifeline. With power surges threatening the feed, he held the camera and the audience, tracking the tornado's path in real time as debris signatures blossomed on screen. By the time the threat passed, his composure had become part of the story — a calm center on a night when seconds mattered, and a performance of duty that likely saved lives.

625. A top vasectomy doctor in Austin, Texas, is named Dick Chop.

626. From February 5 to 8, 2020, botanists Rod and Rachel Saunders appeared on the BBC's Gardeners' World, excitedly searching for rare Lesotho gladioli in South Africa. Just days later, they vanished. Their blood-stained car was found abandoned, and investigators believe they were ambushed in their tent, murdered, and robbed. Their bodies were later discovered in a crocodile-infested river.

627. The 2021 Croatian *Got Talent* audition of singer Roman Bernarda and violinist Bianca Colar devolved into confrontation when they ignored 4 buzzers and scolded the judges. Months afterward, amid enduring

psychosis and substance problems, Roman attacked a fan he misidentified as a thief, killed her, wandered naked outside, and was placed in a secure hospital instead of prison.

628. There's a real hand sanitizer brand called "Maybe You Touched Your Genitals."

629. Stage "buried alive" stunts share a deadly constant: the earth is heavier and faster than the magician. Early trials nearly broke Houdini; in one attempt, he clawed upward through collapsing soil, emerging shaken and gasping, and later dropped plans for a definitive version, conceding that the risk outweighed the trick. Decades on, radio daredevil Bill Shirk tried a burial sealed under dirt and cement. The load crushed his coffin before he fought his way out, bloodied and barely breathing — a survival closer to catastrophe than applause. "The Amazing Joe" never surfaced at all. Using untested materials and working without a real rescue plan, he went under wet cement; the mixture caved in his coffin, and he died within minutes.

The common thread isn't mystery but physics. Soil and concrete don't just press — they flow, they find seams, and they multiply pressure with every added inch. Tiny miscalculations turn final, and the air you think you've banked vanishes faster than panic can rise. The posters promise resurrection; the track record says the ground always wins.

630. One degree of latitude equals approximately 69 miles (about 111 kilometers).

631. During a 2015 Honduran morning show, viewers watched as a glass of water inexplicably slid across the anchor's desk. The host reported feeling a sudden chill at the same moment, sparking viral speculation about possible paranormal activity in the studio.

632. A fire at The Station nightclub in Rhode Island in 2003 killed 100 people and injured over 200. Pyrotechnics ignited flammable insulation, and the building lacked sprinklers or emergency exits.

633. One of history's strangest epidemics hit Tanganyika in 1962, when uncontrollable laughter spread through villages near Lake Victoria, starting at a girls' school and affecting up to thousands of people with fits

of laughter lasting hours or days — a case historians consider a mass psychogenic illness.

634. A live television segment near Smith Mountain Lake, Virginia, on August 26, 2015, ended in tragedy when a former colleague opened fire, killing reporter Alison Parker and cameraman Adam Ward. The interviewee survived. The shooter fled and later died by suicide after a police pursuit, sparking nationwide scrutiny of gun policy and on-air safety.

635. In 2006, Truman Duncan was run over by a train and cut in half — he stayed conscious and called 911, surviving despite massive injuries.

636. During a live Larry King Live segment touring Michael Jackson's Neverland Ranch, viewers spotted a human-shaped shadow crossing a distant hallway — complete with what appeared to be a floor reflection. The eerie figure quickly sparked speculation, with many convinced it was Jackson's ghost haunting his former home. While some dismissed it as a camera crew member or a trick of lighting, the moment became a viral sensation and fuel for ghost-hunting theories.

637. In the U.K., on May 16, 2008, Sabina and Ursula Eriksson stood serenely on the M6 median before suddenly running into traffic — an incident captured by Motorway Cops. Both were hit and survived, then fought medical staff and ranted about organ theft. Authorities released Sabina without a psychiatric hold. The next day, still delusional, she killed a stranger and jumped off a bridge, surviving and later receiving a reduced sentence after a mental-health diagnosis.

12. Murderous Minds & Cult Horrors

Some minds are capable of unimaginable darkness. From unsolved child murders to notorious serial killers and audacious crime lords, these stories reveal cruelty, obsession, and the terrifying extremes of human behavior.

638. For decades, "the Boy in the Box" hurt because he had no name — just a small body in a cardboard bassinet box found in Philadelphia in 1957. In December 2022, DNA and genealogy finally gave him back his identity: 4-year-old Joseph Augustus Zarelli. Police say the homicide case is still open. The identity and motive remain unanswered, even though the child now has a headstone with his name.

639. Robert Bowers opened fire inside Pittsburgh's Tree of Life Synagogue in 2018, killing 11 worshippers and injuring several others. Motivated by white supremacist ideology, he was sentenced to death and is being held under maximum security.

640. Robert Pickton's crimes remain among the most horrifying in Canadian history. A pig farmer from British Columbia, Pickton preyed on vulnerable women — many of them Indigenous and from Vancouver's Downtown Eastside — between 1995 and 2001. He lured them to his farm, where they were murdered and their remains gruesomely disposed of.

Police eventually found chilling evidence on his property: body parts, bloodstains, and remains so thoroughly destroyed that some were believed to have been mixed with ground pork, prompting warnings that meat from his farm might have been contaminated with human flesh. Pickton was charged with dozens of murders, convicted of 6 in 2007, and later admitted to killing 49 women, boasting that he had hoped to make it an even 50.

The case shocked the world and exposed systemic failures in how law enforcement handled cases involving missing Indigenous women. Pickton is now considered one of Canada's most notorious serial killers, his crimes leaving lasting scars on the communities he targeted and fueling national conversations about justice, marginalization, and the dangers of unchecked violence.

641. For months, neighbors complained about a sickening stench in Cleveland, and suspicion fell on a local spot called Ray's Sausage. But the smell wasn't from the restaurant at all — it came from next door, where Anthony Sowell had hidden the decomposing bodies of 11 women inside his home.

642. Pablo Escobar once offered to pay Colombia's entire national debt — estimated at $10 billion at the time — in return for legal immunity. The audacious proposal reflected his immense wealth from cocaine trafficking and his belief that he could buy the state's cooperation, but the government ultimately refused. The offer became emblematic of Escobar's power and his ruthless "plata o plomo" approach, which forced officials to choose between accepting bribes or facing violence.

643. Ottis Toole was a drifter and convicted serial killer whose chilling confessions in the early 1980s stunned investigators. He laughed as he described acts of murder, arson, and cannibalism, calling killing "nothing" and speaking casually about burning cities and draining blood. His lack of remorse and erratic storytelling made him one of the most disturbing figures in American true crime history.

644. Rodney Alcala, a serial predator suspected of killing over 100 people, once appeared on *The Dating Game*. He actually won, but the woman who picked him backed out of the date after meeting him — she said something about him that felt deeply wrong. The decision may have saved her life.

645. Night after night in 2019, exactly at 1:33 a.m., Ellie and Grace in Manchester picked up unsettling calls. The footsteps and whispers soon echoed what was happening in real time. Investigators traced the source to a phone in a ceiling vent and a man living within the ductwork above their apartment.

646. The González Valenzuela sisters, known as "Las Poquianchis," ran a Mexican brothel network where they murdered prostitutes deemed "too old" and wealthy customers for their money. Nearly 100 bodies were

discovered in the 1960s. Two sisters died in prison; one was institutionalized, and one was released.

647. Patrick McNeill left a bar and slipped off the map. Fifty days later, his body surfaced in the East River — but the details didn't sit right with everyone. Some investigators noted decomposition that seemed uneven for a simple drowning, and marks that looked uncomfortably like restraints. Detective Kevin Gannon saw a pattern. McNeill's case, he argued, echoed dozens of other disappearances: young men out drinking, vanishing near water, and later recovered downstream — sometimes in view of a crude smiley face scrawled on a wall or bridge.

From there, the theory hardened into a chilling possibility: not accidents, but coordinated murders. Supporters point to clusters in time and place, similar victim profiles, and recovery sites that feel staged rather than random. The FBI, however, has pushed back for years, calling the drownings tragic but explainable — alcohol, cold water, bad luck — and the smiley faces, nothing more than common graffiti found almost anywhere. Between those 2 readings lies a grim stalemate. McNeill's death sits at the center of it: either the first breadcrumb in a hidden trail of homicides, or the most haunting example of how grief and coincidence can draw a pattern where none was meant to be.

648. Vickie Dawn Jackson, a nurse in North Texas, was linked to a string of suspicious deaths in 2000 and 2001 when patients suddenly developed respiratory distress. Missing vials of the paralytic drug mivacurium and a syringe with residue were discovered, leading to her arrest. She pleaded no contest to multiple murders and is serving a life sentence.

649. Issei Sagawa, the Japanese man who murdered and cannibalized a classmate in France, told his story with a disturbing calm. His soft, almost childlike voice made the gruesome details even more jarring, creating a chilling clash between innocence of tone and horror of content.

650. Despite his violent criminal career, many Americans suffering through the Great Depression saw John Dillinger as a folk hero who robbed banks — widely viewed at the time as corrupt institutions — and outwitted authorities. He reportedly received fan letters, and some even

sent him love notes and money, reinforcing his status as a charismatic outlaw.

651. Javed Iqbal confessed to murdering 100 children in Pakistan and was sentenced to be executed in the exact way he killed his victims — strangled, dismembered, and dissolved in acid. He was found dead in his cell before the sentence could be carried out.

652. After weeks of silent night calls in 2015, Calgary police traced them to a woman named Amanda's own landline and discovered a tampered crawl space beneath her apartment containing a sleeping bag, food, and a burner phone used to tap her line.

653. H.H. Holmes, born Herman Webster Mudgett, is often called America's first serial killer. A medical school graduate who dabbled in grave robbing, Holmes moved to Chicago in the late 1880s and built a labyrinthine hotel later dubbed the "Murder Castle." Complete with trap doors, soundproof rooms, gas lines, and hidden chutes to the basement, it became a death trap for victims — often young women lured by job offers or the excitement of the 1893 World's Fair.

Holmes confessed to more than 200 murders, though he was definitively tied to 9. He dismembered, gassed, or tortured victims, sometimes selling their skeletons to medical schools. Arrested for murdering a business partner and 3 of the man's children, Holmes was hanged in 1896. The Murder Castle became infamous as a symbol of Gilded Age horror, blending true crime with legend — a grim reminder of how America's first documented serial killer turned ambition into monstrosity.

654. John Floyd Thomas Jr., linked through DNA to decades of unsolved murders in Los Angeles, was convicted of killing elderly women and is considered one of the city's most prolific serial killers. He is serving multiple life sentences in maximum security.

655. After murdering John Lennon, Mark David Chapman remained at the scene, pulled out a copy of *The Catcher in the Rye*, and began reading it while waiting for the police to arrive. He later stated he believed the book held the key to his actions and identified with its protagonist, Holden Caulfield, claiming he killed Lennon to preserve the innocence he felt Lennon had betrayed.

656. Jesse James wasn't just a bandit — he was also a master of self-mythologizing. After the Civil War, he wrote letters to newspapers framing himself as a Robin Hood-style rebel fighting Northern oppression. These letters, often signed with flair, helped him gain public sympathy, especially in the former Confederate South, even though there's no evidence he ever shared his loot with the poor. His flair for PR made him one of America's first criminal celebrities.

657. Bonnie Parker and Clyde Barrow robbed banks, stores, and filling stations across the central U.S. during the Great Depression, surviving multiple shootouts before a 1934 police ambush in Louisiana ended their headline-making crime spree.

658. Micajah and Wiley Harpe, better known as the Harpe Brothers, carved their place in history as America's first documented serial killers. Loyalists during and after the American Revolution, they drifted through the lawless frontier of the late 18th century, leaving a trail of terror in their wake. Unlike most outlaws of their time, the Harpes didn't just rob or settle scores — they killed indiscriminately, targeting men, women, and even children with shocking brutality.

Their spree became so notorious that early newspapers labeled them "monsters," and a massive manhunt was launched to stop them. In 1799, Micajah, or "Big Harpe," was captured and decapitated after being fatally wounded; his severed head was mounted on a tree as a grim warning to other criminals. Wiley, or "Little Harpe," escaped capture for years but was eventually arrested and executed in 1804.

659. Ramzi Yousef masterminded the 1993 World Trade Center bombing, which killed 6 people and injured over 1,000. He is serving a life sentence plus 240 years at ADX Florence, a supermax prison known for housing America's most dangerous criminals, in a high-security wing known as "Bombers Row."

660. In the 1950s in Columbia, Missouri, a teen babysitter received repeated calls urging her to "check the children." When the operator traced the line, it led to an upstairs extension inside the house. Police arrived, found no intruder, and confirmed the children were safe — but

the eerie incident helped seed the urban legend that would later inspire countless retellings.

661. In 2007, threatening calls started coming to teenager Jessica Harmon of suburban Chicago as she sat home alone. Police arrived and discovered a man curled in a hallway closet, clutching a prepaid phone; he had spent hours inside, silently watching through the thin slit of the door.

662. Gary Ridgway, the "Green River Killer," spoke about luring women with a frightening lack of emotion. He admitted to showing photos of his young son to gain their trust, a manipulation that helped him carry out dozens of murders without a flicker of remorse.

663. Two brothers playing video games late at night were interrupted by a man with a terrifying smile who handcuffed himself to their window and knocked over 30 times. After calling 911, the man attempted to break into their back door, eventually succeeding and smashing objects in their kitchen while yelling for them. The police arrived just in time to tackle and arrest him. He was later confirmed to be high on meth and looking to rob the house.

664. In 1964, at just 15 years old, Ed Kemper murdered his grandparents in North Fork, California. After being institutionalized and later released, he went on to kill six female college students between 1972 and 1973 in the Santa Cruz area. His final victim was his own mother, whom he murdered in April 1973, performing disturbing acts with her remains. Kemper then drove to Colorado and called police from a phone booth, confessing to the crimes and turning himself in.

665. Dawood Ibrahim, one of the world's most infamous crime lords, rose from the streets of Mumbai to lead D-Company, a sprawling criminal syndicate involved in smuggling, extortion, narcotics, and contract killings. By the 1980s and early 1990s, he had become India's most feared underworld figure, operating with an international reach that blurred the lines between organized crime and terrorism.

Indian authorities link Ibrahim directly to the devastating 1993 Bombay bombings, a coordinated series of explosions that killed over 250 people and injured thousands. The attacks were seen as retaliation for communal violence in India, and Ibrahim was accused of orchestrating them with support from foreign networks. Over the years, he has also been tied to Islamist extremist groups, earning a place on global terrorist watchlists.

Despite Interpol notices and pressure from multiple governments, Ibrahim has evaded capture for decades. He is widely believed to be living under protection in Pakistan, though officials there deny it.

666. In 1888, Jack the Ripper allegedly mailed half of a human kidney preserved in alcohol to a Whitechapel vigilante committee member, boasting that he had eaten the other half. The chilling note, known as the "From Hell" letter, remains one of the Ripper case's most disturbing and mysterious pieces of evidence.

667. Jeffrey Dahmer, the infamous Milwaukee serial killer, tried to create submissive "zombies" by drilling holes into his victims' skulls and injecting hydrochloric acid or boiling water into their brains, hoping to keep them alive but under his control. In one chilling incident, 14-year-old Konerak Sinthasomphone managed to escape, but when neighbors called the police, Dahmer convinced the officers that the boy was his adult boyfriend. They returned Konerak to Dahmer's apartment, where he was murdered soon after.

668. Denise and Kyle, living in St. Louis in 2009, received short-ring calls that replayed their private talks. Investigators traced the line to a second phone in the house and found a prepaid device plus audio equipment stashed in a basement cabinet, but the caller was never identified.

669. Dylann Roof murdered 9 African-American churchgoers in Charleston, South Carolina, in 2015, aiming to incite racial violence. He was convicted on federal hate crime charges and sentenced to death, becoming the first person in the U.S. to receive a federal death penalty for a hate crime.

670. Despite helping orchestrate the 1995 Oklahoma City bombing — one of the deadliest domestic terrorist attacks in U.S. history — Terry Nichols claimed to be a devout Christian and reportedly spent his time in prison reading the Bible and making legal arguments based on religious texts. He filed multiple bizarre lawsuits from prison, including one against prison food, arguing that serving white bread violated his religious beliefs.

671. In 2023, a Kansas babysitter checking under a child's bed — at the child's request — discovered an intruder hiding beneath it. The man, who had previously lived in the home and was under a protection order, had secretly returned and was caught violating that order. What began as a routine monster check turned into a chilling real-life encounter.

672. Pedro López, the "Monster of the Andes," confessed to killing over 100 girls across Colombia, Ecuador, and Peru. He was convicted in 1980 for 110 murders in Ecuador and sentenced to 16 years, the maximum penalty allowed at the time. After serving 14 years, he was released in 1994 and transferred to a psychiatric hospital in Colombia. Four years later, in 1998, doctors declared him sane and fit for release. López vanished shortly after and remains at large. He is suspected of additional killings, and his current whereabouts are unknown.

673. James Marcello, a former leader of the Chicago Outfit, was convicted of racketeering, conspiracy, and several murders tied to the FBI's Operation Family Secrets. He is serving a life sentence at ADX Florence.

674. Khalid Sheikh Mohammed, considered the principal architect of the September 11th terrorist attacks, was captured in Pakistan in March 2003. He has been held at the Guantanamo Bay detention camp since then and faces multiple terrorism-related charges, though his trial has been delayed for years amid complex legal proceedings.

675. Amado Carrillo Fuentes, known as the "Lord of the Skies," died in 1997 while undergoing plastic surgery meant to drastically change his appearance to evade capture. But the story didn't end there — shortly after his death, the 2 surgeons who performed the operation were found murdered, their bodies encased in concrete inside steel drums, sparking conspiracy theories that Carrillo may have faked his death. Some believe he used a double and escaped, with his cartel secretly covering up the switch.

676. In 2022 in Los Angeles, housesitter Tasha received blocked-number calls — "I'm inside, I'm looking at you" — and ran. A follow-up police search uncovered a man hidden behind a false wall panel in a guest room,

where he had set up a miniature surveillance room and made the calls from within.

677. In the U.S., roughly 1 in 3 murders go unsolved, leaving a staggering backlog of cold cases. Since the 1960s, more than 200,000 homicides have remained open.

678. In 2013, a babysitter named Lauren in Kansas City began receiving disturbing phone calls describing her appearance and movements in real time. When police investigated, they discovered a man hiding in the basement — he had been secretly living there for days. Using a burner phone and a cloned version of her number, he made it appear as though the calls were coming from inside the house. Alongside the phone, officers found detailed notes he had taken on her routine.

679. Richard Chase, known as the Vampire of Sacramento, killed 6 people in the 1970s and drank their blood, believing his own blood was turning to powder. Police found cups and utensils coated in blood in his apartment.

680. The Order of the Solar Temple was founded in 1984 by Belgian homeopath Luc Jouret and French neo-Templar Joseph Di Mambro, presenting itself as a secret society modeled after the medieval Knights Templar. Blending apocalyptic prophecy, ritual mysticism, and conspiracy theories, the group claimed its followers were preparing for a spiritual transition to a new world. At its height, it operated lodges across Europe and North America, recruiting well-educated and affluent members drawn to its promise of hidden wisdom.

But behind its esoteric facade, the cult spiraled into violence. In October 1994, members in Switzerland ritually murdered a 3-month-old baby — the child of 2 followers — after leaders declared the infant to be the Antichrist. Soon after, the group carried out a series of coordinated mass suicides and murders, with dozens of members found dead in chalets and compounds in Switzerland and Canada, many dressed in ceremonial robes. Additional deaths followed in 1995 and 1997, cementing the Solar Temple's reputation as one of the most infamous cults of the late 20th century.

Today, French authorities classify the Order of the Solar Temple as an active criminal organization, warning that remnants of its network and ideology still persist. The group remains a grim example of how apocalyptic belief, secrecy, and authoritarian leadership can culminate in tragedy on a massive scale.

681. In 1978, John Wayne Gacy was already hiding the bodies of dozens of young men beneath his house when he briefly brushed shoulders with history. He met First Lady Rosalynn Carter at a public event, smiling for photos while in the middle of a murder spree that would leave 33 victims.

682. James Holmes carried out the 2012 Aurora, Colorado, movie theater shooting, killing 12 people and injuring 70. He received 12 consecutive life sentences and over 3,300 additional years and is currently incarcerated at U.S.P. Allenwood in Pennsylvania.

683. Al Capone built a Prohibition-era bootlegging empire in Chicago and ordered gangland hits — including the St. Valentine's Day Massacre — while cultivating a celebrity image; federal tax charges in 1931 ended his reign and sent him to prison.

684. In 1977, sitting in a jailhouse chair in Colorado, Ted Bundy turned an interview into a performance. He held eye contact too long, flashed easy smiles, and dropped gentle jokes as if he were the most harmless man in the room. The charm worked like camouflage, smoothing over the bars at his back and the mounting suspicions around him. Viewers saw a handsome law student with quick wit and steady nerves — precisely the mask he'd worn to move through crowds, borrow trust, and vanish with victims.

A dozen years later, the showman faltered. On the night before his 1989 execution, Bundy looked drawn and frightened under prison lights, his voice thinner than the swaggering quips of his earlier interviews. He groped for explanations and deflections — at one point blaming violent pornography for "feeding" his obsessions — as crowds gathered outside the prison and news cameras tracked every breath. The contrast was stark: the grinning charm that once disarmed an audience now read as stagecraft, and behind it, for the first time, a man who knew the curtain was finally coming down.

685. Gerard Schaefer, a Florida deputy sheriff, kidnapped and released 2 teenage hitchhikers, later killing 2 more girls. Stories and trophies found in his home linked him to numerous killings, possibly up to 30. He was convicted and stabbed to death in prison in 1995.

686. Despite being the prime suspect in a string of brutal murders in Michigan during the late 1960s, John Norman Collins was never convicted for most of them. He was only tried and convicted for the 1969 murder of Karen Sue Beineman — the last known victim. However, the distinct method and pattern of the killings, timeline, and forensic evidence closely linked him to at least 6 other homicides, all involving young women. Collins, a former fraternity member and literature student, was even suspected of using his charm and knowledge of anatomy to deceive victims, and some believe he may have had an accomplice in at least one of the unsolved cases.

687. In 1992, a clerk in an Indianapolis Payless was executed in the back room; 3 days later, 2 bridal-shop workers in Wichita were shot after hours, and more victims followed in small shops off I-70. Cash drawers were open, but the violence looked methodical, not profit-driven. The shootings paused, then echoed in 1993 along I-35 in Texas with a different caliber; 1 victim survived and described the gunman. Decades on, a 2001 video yielded a look-alike, but no confirmed capture.

688. Dzhokhar Tsarnaev carried out the 2013 Boston Marathon bombing with his brother, killing 3 and injuring hundreds. After a manhunt that ended in his arrest, Tsarnaev was sentenced to death and is currently on federal death row at **ADX Florence**.

689. The Nuwaubian movement, founded by Dwight York in the 1970s, claimed that aborted fetuses live in sewers plotting to take over the world, that Satan's child was born in New York to Jacqueline Kennedy Onassis, and that aliens will one day take 144,000 chosen people away in a flying saucer. York is serving a 135-year sentence for racketeering, child sex trafficking, and molestation.

690. Richard Ramirez, known as the "Night Stalker," reveled in his dark reputation. In court, he declared himself evil and proud of it, flashing a

cold stare that unsettled even seasoned observers. His open embrace of Satanism only deepened the terror surrounding his brutal crimes.

691. Despite being one of the most powerful mob bosses in American history, Luciano made a secret deal with the U.S. government during World War 2. While imprisoned for running a prostitution ring, he offered his criminal network's help in protecting New York's docks from Axis sabotage. In return for this wartime cooperation — known as Operation Underworld — his sentence was commuted, though he was deported to Italy instead of being released in the U.S.

692. John Gotti earned the nickname "The Teflon Don" after repeatedly beating charges in high-profile trials during the 1980s, as none of the criminal indictments seemed to stick — just like food sliding off a Teflon pan. Prosecutors struggled to convict him, as key witnesses vanished, jurors were bribed, and evidence mysteriously disappeared. His confident swagger, flashy suits, and media charm only reinforced the image of an untouchable mafia boss, cementing his celebrity status even as bodies piled up behind the scenes.

693. Jean-Bernard Lasnaud, a French broker notorious for skirting arms embargoes, marketed surplus weapons — including jets — through glossy catalogs and a website from his luxury base, becoming a symbol of modern gray-market dealing before arrests and seizures caught up with him.

694. Recent research has reinforced what criminologists have long suspected: psychopathy is one of the strongest predictors of reoffending. Studies conducted between 2021 and 2024 found that individuals who scored high on psychopathy assessments not only reoffend at higher rates than other offenders but also tend to do so more quickly. A trend that held true across psychopathy subtypes, genders, and a wide range of crimes, from violent assaults to financial fraud.

The risk becomes even more pronounced when psychopathy is paired with additional factors like substance abuse or sexual deviance, creating a dangerous profile of offenders who are resistant to rehabilitation. These findings confirm psychopathy's reputation as one of the most challenging traits in criminal psychology, often associated with shallow emotions, manipulation, and a lack of remorse. For law enforcement and mental health professionals, the data underscores the difficulty of predicting and preventing crimes committed by psychopathic offenders.

695. Sirhan Bishara Sirhan assassinated Senator Robert F. Kennedy on June 5, 1968, in Los Angeles. Initially sentenced to death, his sentence was commuted to life in prison in 1972. Although he was granted parole in 2021, the decision was blocked by California's governor. He remains incarcerated at Richard J. Donovan Correctional Facility.

696. Albert Fish, known as the "Gray Man" and the "Brooklyn Vampire," once sent a chilling letter to the family of 10-year-old Grace Budd, a girl he murdered and cannibalized. In it, he described luring her to an abandoned house, killing her, and cooking her body with onions and carrots. The letter was so graphic that even hardened detectives were horrified — and it ultimately led to Fish's capture in 1934.

697. Eric Rudolph orchestrated the 1996 Centennial Olympic Park bombing in Atlanta, killing one person directly and injuring more than 100. He committed additional bombings in Georgia and Alabama before being captured and is serving multiple life sentences at ADX Florence.

698. Danilo Cavalcante, a Brazilian national, was convicted of murdering his ex-girlfriend in Pennsylvania and escaped prison in September 2023, prompting a large-scale manhunt. He was recaptured and returned to maximum security.

699. In 1920, Charles Ponzi became a household name by convincing thousands of Americans he had discovered a brilliant way to get rich. He claimed he could exploit price differences in international postal reply coupons — small vouchers used for international postage — to deliver investors returns of 50% in just 45 days. People flocked to him with their savings, and Ponzi paid early investors exactly as promised, building a reputation as a financial genius.

But behind the scenes, there was no fortune-making system. Ponzi wasn't actually investing in coupons at all; he was simply using money from new investors to pay the old ones, creating the illusion of endless profit. At the height of his scheme, he was raking in millions of dollars, out-earning some of the largest banks in Boston, and living lavishly while newspapers praised his financial wizardry.

When the truth unraveled, Ponzi's empire collapsed almost overnight, costing investors millions and landing him in prison. The scandal was so notorious that his name became forever attached to this kind of fraud — the Ponzi scheme — a swindle that still thrives a century later, proving how greed and trust can be manipulated with devastating ease.

700. Danny Rolling, the "Gainesville Ripper," staged his murders for maximum horror. In one case, he placed a victim's severed head on a bookshelf and arranged the body in a seated position. The grotesque posing was meant to terrify anyone who discovered the scene.

701. Carl Panzram was a violent drifter who claimed in his autobiography to have murdered 22 people, though only 5 killings were confirmed. Active internationally in the 1910s–1920s, he was known for his hatred of humanity and violent outbursts. After murdering a prison foreman while serving time, he was executed in 1930.

702. In 2010, 25-year-old Michael Bray from Maryland killed his mother with a ceremonial sword during a psychotic episode. He was later diagnosed with schizophrenia and found not guilty by reason of mental disease. The court committed him to a secure psychiatric facility.

13. Secrets, Lies & Collective Madness

Some ideas bend reality, twist logic, or spark full-blown cultural panic. Cosmic theories, supernatural myths, and mind-bending thought experiments push the limits of what people believe — and reveal how quickly curiosity can slip into obsession.

703. Eternal recurrence suggests infinite time guarantees every event repeats infinitely. Universes may cyclically collapse and reform, ensuring infinite identical versions of your life and countless variations.

704. 'Oumuamua was our first known visitor from another star — thin, fast, and tumbling in a way we didn't expect. Its brief pass left only fragmentary data, and scientists argued over what it was as it sped away. By the time the debate got going, it was already out of the Solar System, leaving more questions than answers.

705. Roko's Basilisk is a thought experiment in which a future superintelligent AI punishes those who didn't help create it. Now that you know about it, you're theoretically "on its list," highlighting fears of AI dominance.

706. Charles Fort, born in 1874 and died in 1932, was a writer who compiled reports of unexplained events — fish and frogs falling from the sky, strange lights, teleportation tales — and insisted they should be logged rather than dismissed. His books gave rise to the term "Fortean," now shorthand for interest in the anomalous.

707. Nephilim turn ancient verses into a mythic bloodline — fallen angels mingling with mortals to spawn giants. Goliath becomes just one in a chart of erased tribes and hidden hybrids. Some modern takes imagine the remnants still lurking in remote places, where the divine and the earthly still blur.

708. Gorillas were long considered mythical creatures akin to Bigfoot until explorers and naturalists confirmed their existence in the mid-1800s. Early European depictions described them as monstrous, but expeditions revealed them to be intelligent primates.

709. Apocalyptic prophecies in Christian tradition have long fueled conspiracy theories about the Antichrist, a leader said to unite the world under tyranny before the end times. Across history, figures like Frederick II, Saladin, Peter the Great, Pope John XXII, Napoleon Bonaparte, Benito Mussolini, and Adolf Hitler have all been branded as the Antichrist. Even modern politicians, such as Barack Obama, have faced similar accusations.

710. Some scientists and philosophers argue that we may be living in a simulation — a digital universe created by an advanced civilization. The logic is statistical: if future societies develop the power to run countless simulations of reality, the odds suggest we're far more likely to be inside one of those simulations than in the "base" universe. Proponents speculate that subtle clues, like limits in mathematical constants such as Pi, might expose the boundaries of the system, revealing that our universe runs on finite hardware precision rather than infinite math.

Though unproven, the idea has gained traction among physicists and tech thinkers, raising questions about free will, existence, and the nature of reality itself. If true, every star, atom, and memory could be nothing more than code — and the search for meaning may be less about understanding the universe and more about understanding its programmer.

711. "Lost civilizations" aren't always about mythical cities — they're often real places we haven't relocated or verified on the map. Ancient texts point one way while the ground offers little proof, leaving gaps that take years to close. Each new discovery reminds us how incomplete our record is. If we can misplace a metropolis, it raises the question of what else history filed in the wrong drawer.

712. Astral projection claims to let the self float free from the body, seeing without eyes. Some hospitals have placed hidden symbols on rooftops in hopes of testing these out-of-body reports. While believers speak of spirit footprints and remote interference, skeptics point to one stubborn flaw: no one has been able to replicate it on demand.

713. Sailors describe pale, whale-sized humanoids — ningen — gliding through polar seas and luring crews with eerie sounds. Variants of the same figure appear in cultures that likely never compared notes,

suggesting either a shared source or a shared need. The ocean keeps reflecting our fears back at us.

714. In 2022, Google engineer Blake Lemoine claimed that artificial intelligence chatbots were sentient, fueling fears of uncontrollable AI. By 2025, 20% of Americans believed AI may already think independently. Experts warn sentient AI could reshape ethics, jobs, and power structures, sparking debates about AI rights, control, and the risk of humanity creating "superior beings."

715. The High-frequency Active Auroral Research Program is officially a scientific project studying the ionosphere, but it has become a focal point for conspiracy theories linking it to weather manipulation and natural disasters. Critics suggest its capabilities could be used for control under the guise of research, fueling suspicion. Regardless of intent, the image of powerful antennas targeting the sky has made it a lasting source of public unease.

716. Space-is-fake claims lower the ceiling on reality, recasting the night sky as a projection. Stars become pixels or curtains, and distrust is solved by shrinking the stage. The bigger the doubt, the smaller the universe has to become.

717. SeaLab put scientists on the seafloor until an accident killed a diver and the program shuttered. Officially, the risks outweighed the rewards; unofficially, some think the research just got classified. The ocean is perfect for work that prefers no witnesses.

718. In 2016, the "creepy clown" thing spread from city to city with no ringleader — just rumors, costumes, and social media feeding on itself. It kicked off with unsubstantiated reports in South Carolina and then popped up across the U.S. and abroad, mostly pranks and copycats rather than organized threats. Schools and police fielded floods of calls about masked clowns (sometimes with knives), retailers yanked scary masks, and a few people were arrested in scattered incidents. And then — almost as fast as it started — it fizzled, the classic arc of a social contagion where fear syncs strangers faster than any switchboard.

719. The Tartaria theory claims there was a vast, advanced empire erased from history, with a "mudflood" said to have buried its grand

architecture. Historians clarify that "Tartary" was simply a historical term for Central Asia, and the buildings often cited match architectural styles and urban development from the 1700s and 1800s. Online, the myth reflects distrust in mainstream history and fascination with a romanticized hidden past.

720. Project Serpo claims 12 U.S. military personnel traveled to an alien planet in the Zeta Reticuli system in 1965 after the Roswell crash. According to leaked emails, they lived among extraterrestrials for 13 years, with only 8 returning. Critics cite inconsistencies and suspect a disinformation campaign, but Serpo remains popular in UFO circles.

721. The Boltzmann brain paradox argues it's statistically likelier for a single brain with false memories to form via quantum fluctuations than an entire universe. You could be a lone brain hallucinating existence.

722. Experiments show brain activity precedes conscious decision-making, suggesting free will may be an illusion. Consciousness could merely observe choices already made by neural processes.

723. Some interpret *Back to the Future* as coded prophecy, pointing to clocks, timestamps, and Twin Pines as hidden references to 9/11 — an example of apophenia, where the mind finds patterns in coincidence, especially after trauma. Similarly, dowsing endures as a folk method of detection, with believers sensing real signals from the earth and skeptics attributing it to unconscious muscle movement. Both reveal how belief often survives on compelling stories more than consistent proof.

724. Back in 1996, at a GM plant in Anderson, Indiana, a few workers swore they saw little 6 to 8-inch gray-red "squids" (or about 15 to 20 centimeters) wriggling in an oil-sludge pit. Nobody got a verified specimen — one jarred sample supposedly vanished — and later clean-outs didn't turn up anything like it. There are no photos, no papers, just retellings on cryptid corners of the internet.

725. In the 1970s, the CIA developed a "heart attack gun" that fired toxin-coated darts, causing undetectable deaths. The darts melted inside the body, leaving only a small red mark, and were meant to simulate natural heart attacks. The weapon was revealed in a 1975 Senate hearing, but its fate remains unknown.

726. A viral TikTok by a gravedigger claiming that coffins felt suspiciously light has fueled theories about missing bodies, organ harvesting, and reused burial equipment. Historical practices like body-snatching for medical research add weight to fears of hidden exploitation. Recent cases, such as a 2025 Italian gravedigger arrested for removing corpses from crowded cemeteries, show that grave reuse still happens. Critics suspect funeral industries may secretly recycle graves or mishandle remains, especially in densely populated areas.

727. For the ancient Greeks, Thule was the name for the farthest north anyone could imagine — a misty place where marvels and monsters were said to live. Later writers tried to pin it down on a real map, pointing to Iceland, Norway, or sometimes nowhere at all. Over time, it turned into a symbol of the extreme north, with endless nights and strange lights in the sky. What began as a blank spot on the map grew into a lasting, romantic shadow of the unknown.

728. Fluoride has been added to public water supplies for decades to prevent tooth decay, but critics claim it's a deliberate tool to dull intelligence and increase compliance. Some studies link high fluoride exposure to reduced IQ, while mainstream scientists call water fluoridation a major public health success with minimal risks.

729. In the lore, Rosicrucians are a hidden brotherhood that fused Christian mysticism with secret "scientific" arts — alchemy, astrology, and sacred geometry — to steer history from behind the curtain. Their origin story traces to a vault of Christian Rosenkreuz and a chain of "manifestos" that seeded sleeper cells across Europe, each working quiet reforms in religion, medicine, and politics. The current supposedly runs under later fraternities: Masonic degrees, symbols like the rose and cross, and ritual blueprints are said to be Rosicrucian hand-me-downs. Power travels through graded initiations, passwords, and veiled diagrams; knowledge is the engine, and moral refinement the brake.

730. RAND Corporation, founded in 1946, advised on early satellites, nuclear strategy, and Cold War doctrine; detractors dub it a hidden architect of U.S. power. Conspiracy versions say RAND steers a technocratic "new world order," tolerating massive casualties in nuclear scenarios. Public records show influence, but not the omnipotence alleged.

731. People who take DMT often talk about meeting "machine elves" — beings that act both like curious scientists and mischievous pranksters. The patterns in these reports hint at a shared state of mind rather than the same exact vision, but the encounters feel unmistakably other. Whether they're independent entities or just creations of the brain, many who experience them come back convinced they've stepped through a door — real or not, it leaves a mark.

732. Skinwalker Ranch in Utah is steeped in Ute legends of skinwalkers — shape-shifting witches — and is infamous for modern paranormal reports, including UFOs, glowing orbs, cattle mutilations without blood, and tracks that mysteriously vanish. From 1994 to 1996, ranch owners Terry and Gwen Sherman described encounters with bullet-resistant wolves and disappearing dogs. Later, billionaire Robert Bigelow's National Institute for Discovery Science investigated, recording strange lights, odd footprints, and sudden soil disturbances, though conclusive evidence remained elusive, cementing the ranch's reputation as a hotspot for unexplained phenomena.

733. What people call the "Hooton Plan" traces back to a 1943 newspaper piece by Harvard anthropologist Earnest A. Hooton, bluntly titled "Breed War Strain Out of Germans." It was an opinion article — not government policy — suggesting postwar steps like breaking up Germany, long occupation, and encouraging immigration and intermarriage to dilute militant nationalism, ideas that read today as eugenic and ugly. Even at the time, scholars pushed back, and there's no evidence any such "plan" was ever adopted.

734. TikTok creator Andrew Dawson went viral in 2022 after filming a supposed "giant" on a Canadian mountain. He later claimed he was stalked by government agents, retracted his videos under pressure, and posted cryptic warnings before returning to normal content. Months later, his sudden death, ruled a suicide, sparked speculation that he was silenced. Fans link his story to the Men in Black and whistleblower cover-ups.

735. Reports of "fish rain" describe animals falling from the sky in places where they don't belong. The most common explanation involves waterspouts or strong winds lifting small creatures from bodies of water and

carrying them over land. Many cases fit that model, though some details remain hard to verify. The phenomenon endures because it turns ordinary weather into something strange and memorable.

736. "Birds aren't real" satirically alleges that birds were replaced by surveillance drones that "recharge" on power lines. It's intentionally absurd but works as commentary on mass surveillance and how confident claims can sway people. Its popularity comes from memes more than evidence.

737. United Airlines Flight 93 became a symbol of resistance on September 11, 2001. Hijacked as part of Al-Qaeda's coordinated attacks, the plane never reached its intended target — believed to be either the White House or U.S. Capitol — because passengers fought back, forcing it to crash into a field in Shanksville, Pennsylvania, killing all 44 onboard but saving countless lives.

Conspiracy theories soon emerged, claiming the U.S. military shot the jet down, citing reports of low-flying aircraft, missile-like sounds, and debris found miles from the crash site. Others alleged staged phone calls or suggested a different plane crashed. However, multiple investigations, including the 9/11 Commission Report, found no evidence supporting these claims, concluding that passengers' bravery prevented further devastation.

738. 19th-century newspapers frequently reported giant human skeletons allegedly sent to the Smithsonian, sparking theories of a cover-up to protect evolutionary science. Most finds were hoaxes or misidentified animal bones, like the infamous 1869 Cardiff Giant hoax, yet stories of suppressed giant skeletons remain popular among fringe researchers.

739. The Mandela Effect refers to shared false memories — like misquoting "No, I am your father" or remembering the "Berenstein" Bears instead of "Berenstain." Psychologists attribute it to memory errors reinforced by social influence, while others speculate about parallel timelines. It's fascinating because it challenges our trust in collective memory.

740. Simulation theory suggests that our reality might be a programmed construct — a kind of digital illusion — where atoms behave like code, and glitches such as déjà vu or strange coincidences could be signs of

system errors or backend updates. Supporters argue that the universe's inconsistencies hint at a deeper design we were never meant to fully understand. It reframes reality's oddities as clues, not coincidences.

741. Rogue waves, once thought to be sailors' tales, were proven real in 1995 when an 84-foot (25.6-meter) wave struck the Draupner oil platform in Norway. These massive waves, often double the height of surrounding swells, are powerful enough to sink large ships, and scientists estimate that roughly 10 rogue waves exist worldwide at any moment.

742. Genocide denial tends to split into 2 lanes: governments dodging responsibility, and segments of the public recasting well-documented atrocities as hoaxes or "overblown." The tactics are familiar — euphemisms ("civil conflict"), number games, cherry-picked archives, whataboutism, attacking witnesses, and hiring partisan "experts" to muddy the water. The stakes aren't academic: denial shapes reparations, borders, school curricula, and the safety of targeted communities. The counterweight is also consistent — court rulings, survivor testimony, forensic work, and broad scholarly consensus — but the fight over memory keeps going long after the shooting stops.

743 The Montauk Project conspiracy claims that Camp Hero, a decommissioned Air Force base in Montauk, New York, was the site of secret U.S. experiments involving mind control, time travel, and even alien contact. Popularized by Preston Nichols's 1992 book *The Montauk Project: Experiments in Time*, it lacks evidence but remains a cult legend — so influential it inspired *Stranger Things*.

744. The idea of "Illuminati blood banks" takes real longevity fads and pushes them into the shadows, imagining the rich tapping into youth blood as if it were a secret pipeline. Experimental transfusions and anti-aging treatments turn into a ritual of modern vampirism in these stories.

745. Some conspiracy theorists argue that the sinking of the *Titanic* was orchestrated by banker J.P. Morgan to eliminate wealthy rivals who opposed the creation of the Federal Reserve. Morgan, who owned White Star Line, had booked a luxury suite but canceled at the last minute, while Benjamin Guggenheim, Isidor Straus, and John Jacob Astor died in the disaster.

746. The Philosopher's Stone isn't just a myth about making gold — it's a metaphor for transformation itself. Alchemists weren't just chasing riches; they were searching for rules to reshape the world, long before chemistry wrote its formulas. The legend lives on because the desire to refine and improve never dies.

747. Vampire legends emerged from a blend of folklore and misunderstood realities — like plagues, premature burials, and bodies that decayed unusually. In some old cemeteries, physical evidence of these fears remains: corpses found with stakes through the chest, bricks in the mouth, or limbs bound to prevent rising. The myth endures because it offers a vivid explanation for death and the unknown — turning fear into something with a face and teeth.

748. Investigations into 9/11 revealed that the CIA and FBI repeatedly missed opportunities to intercept the hijackers despite multiple warnings. Known terrorists entered the U.S. freely, took flight lessons, and raised red flags that were ignored, including an FBI alert about Zacarias Moussaoui's suspicious training just weeks before the attacks. Even when suspects like Ziad Jarrah were detained abroad, they were released and later piloted planes on 9/11. These failures have led some to suspect negligence, cover-ups, or a deliberate choice not to stop the plot.

749. The Patterson–Gimlin "massacre" theory reinterprets the famous Bigfoot footage as the aftermath of a hunt rather than a chance encounter. Supporters point to alleged blood traces and rushed camerawork as signs of a staged farewell, arguing that the creature's disappearance since then can be explained by its death. It's a somber reinterpretation that keeps the legend alive by imagining it ended that day.

750. Dolphins are considered highly intelligent, capable of advanced sonar communication and emotional connection with humans. Dolphin-assisted therapy is said to help conditions like autism, cerebral palsy, and tumors, while Russian midwife Igor Charkovsky claimed dolphin-assisted births in the 1970s produced exceptionally gifted children. These births reportedly involved dolphins calming mothers and newborns with sonar, resulting in IQs above 150. However, there's no scientific proof, and only one official dolphin birthing center exists today.

751. The Large Hadron Collider drew wild speculation that it might tear reality, even as physicists used it to confirm the Higgs boson. Glitches and oddities around the project were recast as warnings in popular stories, feeding black-hole and timeline fears. The idea persists partly because the machine is immense and the stakes feel cinematic, even though its actual results are firmly scientific.

752. The "sixth extinction" isn't a distant scenario — it's already underway. Earth has endured 5 mass extinctions, and this time human activity — deforestation, climate warming, and pervasive chemical pollution — is driving it. The stakes aren't only about survival but about who is included when we say "we," and how broadly we extend that circle to other species.

753. Los Angeles camouflages its oil rigs in pastel shells and faux office buildings. Behind drywall and glass, derricks churn quietly, dressed like reception lobbies or clock towers. It's an architectural misdirection: if you can't erase industry, you disguise it until it blends in with the brand.

754. Project Blue Beam is a conspiracy theory claiming NASA plans to use holograms, staged earthquakes, and mind-control technology to fake an alien invasion or global religious event, paving the way for a one-world government. First proposed in the 1990s by Serge Monast — who later died of a reported heart attack — the theory remains unsupported by evidence but thrives online, fueled by viral videos of sky anomalies and fears of technological manipulation.

755. Admiral Byrd's Antarctic expedition ended with honors and a sudden silence, which helped fuel enduring myths. Tales of hidden Nazi bases and entrances to "Agartha" grew from the gaps, turning the ice into a symbol of concealed truths. When official records go quiet, speculation tends to fill the void.

756. Operation Fishbowl was a series of high-altitude nuclear tests conducted by the U.S. in 1962, designed to observe how nuclear detonations would interact with the upper atmosphere. Missiles carrying warheads were launched into the ionosphere, creating artificial auroras and electromagnetic effects. Though officially documented, the tests remain unsettling in scope and intent — highlighting that some of the most surreal experiments in history weren't hidden, just officially planned.

757. Pantheism erases the line between God and the world, saying they are the same thing. The sacred isn't elsewhere; it's in breath, stone, and supernova alike. It treats divinity as woven into ordinary matter. The result is a theology that keeps its hands on the world rather than above it.

758. The "dead internet theory" says bots and AI now generate most online content, making discourse hollow since approximately 2016. Critics cite platform monetization and recommendation loops driving sameness, not a literal bot takeover. It resonates because online spaces often feel less human.

759. In 1978, 22-year-old single mother Yaeko Taguchi vanished after leaving her Tokyo workplace, later revealed to have been abducted by North Korean agents to train spies. Japan has confirmed 17 abductions from 1977 to 1983, though evidence suggests up to 800 victims, with North Korea providing fake remains and refusing full accountability.

760. Francis Leavy's ghostly handprint on a firehouse window became a local legend after he died in the line of duty. No amount of scrubbing, cleaning agents, or time could erase it — until, they say, a child with a newspaper finally did. Whether true or not, the story lingers because some imprints feel chosen — not accidental.

14. Strange Events & Gruesome Fates

History is full of moments that shock, confuse, or downright horrify. From battles that seemed haunted to bizarre customs and deadly experiments, reality often proves stranger — and darker — than fiction.

761. Rome didn't pass power from a living emperor to his biological son until 180 BC, when Commodus succeeded Marcus Aurelius. Before that, emperors usually adopted adult heirs — chosen more for politics than blood. It was dynasty by design — not by DNA.

762. During World War 1, German troops attempted to seize the Osowiec Fortress from Russian control. In one of the most disturbing battles, the Germans released chlorine gas, expecting to wipe out the Russians. With no proper gas masks, Russian soldiers used urine-soaked rags in a futile attempt to filter the poison. Many died, but the survivors — blistered, bleeding, and coughing up lungs — still launched a counterattack. The Germans, terrified by what seemed like undead troops rising from the dead, fled. Though most Russians perished later, their stand became legendary as "The Attack of the Dead Men."

763. The word "quarantine" comes from the Venetian quarantina, meaning 40 days. Ships had to wait offshore during outbreaks, hoping time would kill the disease. It was early public health, measured in patience.

764 The title of "world's largest city" has passed like a crown through empires. Alexandria reigned in 1 BCE, followed by Nanjing, then Córdoba, Beijing, and now Tokyo. Size follows power, and power shifts with time.

765. In the brutal siege of Stalingrad, Soviet troops held Pavlov's House for nearly 2 months. German forces threw wave after wave at the single building, suffering more losses there than in the entire fall of Paris. One building became a fortress — and a symbol of Soviet grit.

766. Around 1800, nearly 40% of English brides were already pregnant when they walked down the aisle. Marriage often came after conception, not before. The bump in the belly was just part of the ceremony.

767. In 1971, psychologist Philip Zimbardo ran the Stanford Prison Experiment, in which students played the roles of guards and prisoners. The experiment spiraled out of control when guards began abusing prisoners. The study's methods and ethics remain highly controversial.

768. In medieval warfare, the command "Cry havoc!" was no rallying cry — it meant soldiers could break formation and loot at will. If shouted too soon, it risked chaos that could cost the army the battle. Because of its danger, only a commander could authorize the words, and using them without orders was strictly forbidden.

769. Dick Turpin, the infamous highwayman, was living under the alias John Palmer when he drew attention — not for theft, but for shooting a neighbor's gamecock and making violent threats. That minor act of aggression led to his arrest and eventual identification. In the end, it wasn't his crimes on the road that exposed him, but a careless display of cruelty.

770. Britain's last conviction under the Witchcraft Act came in 1943, when Scottish medium Helen Duncan was jailed. Officials feared her séances might leak wartime secrets. The law targeted fraud, but fear of spirits lingered far beyond superstition.

771. In 1798, Britain's prime minister got into such a heated argument with a fellow Member of Parliament that they met for a pistol duel on Putney Common. Both men missed their shots and then calmly returned to Parliament.

772. During World War 2, the Nazis compiled a "Black Book" listing thousands of names, occupations, and addresses in Britain — targets for arrest if an invasion succeeded. The invasion never came, and the book surfaced after the war like a plan frozen in time. It stands as a reminder of how bureaucracy can organize imagined victories into neat lists, even when history takes a different path.

773. Frank Bourne, the last surviving defender of Rorke's Drift, died on Victory in Europe Day (VE Day) in 1945 at the age of 91. He lived long enough to witness the world go from colonial skirmishes to global war. One soldier, 2 centuries, and a front-row seat to history's violent arc.

774. Rejected by the army because they were women, Flora Murray and Louisa Garrett Anderson built an all-female hospital in 1915. It soon earned a reputation as Britain's best surgical center for wounded soldiers.

775. The only ancient Roman statue to survive outside for centuries is the bronze of Marcus Aurelius on horseback. Mistaken for Constantine, it dodged destruction during medieval purges. Today, the original rests safely indoors — but its legacy still rides on.

776. Pope Pius XII died in 1958 and requested not to be embalmed traditionally. His physician used an experimental method that caused his body to decompose rapidly during the funeral. His corpse turned green, and his chest collapsed in front of mourners.

777. In 1820, the town of Salem, Massachusetts — known for its notorious 17th-century witch trials — put tomatoes on trial. At the time, many believed the fruit to be poisonous. Colonel Robert Gibbon Johnson ate a full basket of tomatoes in public to prove otherwise and didn't die. The trial ended, and tomatoes were redeemed.

778. Hitler's famous toothbrush mustache wasn't a fashion choice at first — it was survival. During World War 1, he trimmed down a fuller style so his gas mask would seal properly. The practical cut stuck, becoming the unsettling signature the world remembers.

779. In Puritan England, Parliament turned the last Wednesday of each month into a national fast day. That included December 25th — meaning Christmas was effectively cancelled. By 1647, they banned it outright, and it stayed that way until the monarchy returned in 1660.

780. In parts of Scotland and Ulster, brides were once "blackened" before their weddings — coated in soot, mud, and feathers. The messy ritual was meant to ward off evil spirits and bring good luck. It was chaos by design, and a blessing wrapped in filth.

781. Richard the Lionheart ruled England for 10 years, from 1189 to 1199, but spent only about 6 months on its soil. He barely spoke the language and saw the kingdom mostly as a source of money for his crusades.

782. King Henry, who reigned from 1100 to 1135, responded to his brother Robert Curthose's defiance with brutal retaliation. He had Robert's 2 granddaughters blinded and mutilated. Their mother later tried to assassinate Henry but missed and escaped by leaping into a moat. It was a violent episode in the struggle for power within the Norman dynasty.

783. In medieval France in the year 1386, a pig was arrested, imprisoned, and put on trial for allegedly killing a child. It was found guilty and executed. While not entirely unheard of in the Middle Ages — animals were occasionally tried for crimes — the absurdity of staging a courtroom drama over a pig remains mind-boggling.

784. Hitler's half-nephew, William Patrick Hitler, turned against his infamous uncle. He moved to America, wrote *Why I Hate My Uncle*, and joined the U.S. Navy to fight in World War 2.

785. On September 8, 1944, Bulgaria found itself in a geopolitical paradox. Still formally at war with the U.S. and the U.K. from 1941, it had just been attacked by the Soviet Union days earlier — and, in a desperate pivot, declared war on Nazi Germany the same day. One small kingdom now stood, on paper, against all the great powers at once.

The moment was the whiplash peak of a year of reversals: an Axis ally that never fought the Soviet Union now faced Red Army troops on its border; a monarchy trying to save itself by switching sides; an army suddenly turning its guns on yesterday's "ally." Within 24 hours, a coup would topple the government and Bulgaria would realign, but for that single day, it was a nation at war with everyone — perhaps the loneliest position any state has ever occupied.

786. In 1820, conman Gregor MacGregor sold plots of land in a country he had invented, calling it Poyais — supposedly located on the coast of present-day Honduras. Settlers arrived to find jungle, disease, and no civilization — just empty promises. Many died, but MacGregor kept printing brochures and collecting cash.

787. During World War 2, French bakers quietly joined the Resistance by hiding messages and supplies inside baguettes. Flour, crust, and sabotage passed right under Nazi noses. Breakfast became a weapon in plain sight.

788. During Prohibition, Americans weren't allowed to make, sell, or transport alcohol — but oddly enough, drinking it at home was still perfectly legal. So if you had a well-stocked stash before the ban kicked in, you were in the clear. For some, the speakeasy was just their living room, and the party never really had to stop.

789. In 1976, Egypt gave Ramesses II a modern passport so his mummy could fly to Paris for conservation. France greeted him with military honors, treated a damaging fungus, confirmed arthritis and battle injuries, and then stamped him home.

790. Germany's November 9 is no ordinary date — it's a magnet for turning points. In one century, it marked the fall of monarchs, failed coups, a pogrom, and the collapse of the Berlin Wall. A single day tangled in both tragedy and transformation.

791. Jesse Owens sprinted to Olympic glory in 1936 wearing shoes crafted by 2 German brothers, Rudolf and Adi Dassler. After World War 2, the brothers split, turning rivalry into legacy — Rudolf founded Puma, while Adi built Adidas. The modern sportswear industry was born out of a family feud.

792. In early modern England, families brewed "groaning ale" as soon as labor began. The mother and midwife drank it during childbirth, and afterward, the leftover ale was poured over the newborn. Folk tradition met sterilization — in a pint glass.

793. Queen Elizabeth I had a serious sweet tooth, especially for sugar — which was a luxury in her time. But without modern dentistry, that indulgence took a toll: her teeth darkened with decay, a fate she shared with many nobles of the era. Her royal smile may have been regal, but it definitely wasn't pearly white.

794. The death of Edward II, who reigned from 1307 to 1327, remains surrounded by uncertainty. While the infamous tale of a red-hot poker used in his murder has endured for centuries, historians widely believe it was a fabrication by political enemies.

795. Neolithic villagers at Skara Brae had indoor drainage systems linked to each stone house, and the Minoan palace at Knossos featured a

flushing toilet. Thousands of years before modern plumbing, ancient engineers were already channeling waste and water with surprising skill.

796. In 1759, during the siege of Madras, British forces accidentally fired on the French headquarters. They followed up with a formal apology — and the French politely accepted. For a moment, manners paused the musket fire.

797. Between 1348 and 1350, the Black Death killed up to 60% of Europe's population. In some cities, quarantined victims fought guards and escaped, causing riots and chaos. Many who fled were attacked on sight as potential plague carriers.

798. On April 26, 1986, Reactor No. 4 at the Chernobyl Nuclear Power Plant in Soviet Ukraine exploded during a late-night safety test gone wrong, unleashing one of the worst nuclear disasters in history. The explosion and fires released massive amounts of radioactive material, contaminating large swaths of Europe. Nearby towns, including Pripyat, were evacuated as residents fled with only what they could carry. Dozens died from acute radiation sickness in the immediate aftermath, while long-term cancers and health effects still haunt the region.

799. At the funeral of U.S. President Andrew Jackson in 1845, his pet African grey parrot had to be removed from the ceremony because it kept loudly swearing and disrupting the mourners. Apparently, the bird had picked up the foul vocabulary from its late owner.

800. Of Churchill's iconic World War 2 speeches, only "Their Finest Hour" aired in his voice at the time. The rest were read by actors on the radio; he re-recorded them years later, in 1949. That gravelly voice we all hear in our heads? Partly postwar imagination.

801. In 1958, the tallest tsunami ever recorded struck Lituya Bay in Alaska — and it was nothing short of jaw-dropping. Triggered by a massive rockslide, the wave surged an incredible 1,720 feet (524 meters) up the surrounding cliffs, shaving off trees like a giant razor. The scars it carved into the landscape still tower high above the water, a reminder of just how wild nature can get.

802. "OK" started as a tongue-in-cheek Boston abbreviation for "oll korrect" in the 1830s. It caught on during Martin Van Buren's presidential campaign — he was nicknamed "Old Kinderhook." What began as a pun is now the most universally recognized word on Earth.

803. When the telephone was new, Alexander Graham Bell thought people should answer with a bold "Ahoy!" — yes, like a ship captain. But Thomas Edison had another idea: "Hello." He pushed for it hard, and eventually, "hello" stuck. If Bell had gotten his way, we might all sound like pirates every time we picked up the phone.

804. Roman engineers built their roads to last — layered with stone, cambered for drainage, and straight as an arrow. Many still lie beneath modern highways, including the Via Appia, which still carries cars today. In a sense, the Romans gave the world not just roads but also its first traffic jams.

805. When forks were first introduced to Italy in the 11th century, religious leaders condemned them as "artificial hands" and declared them offensive to God. Although not officially banned, some Catholic clergy publicly denounced their use.

806. A small French village made headlines in 1954 when it officially banned flying saucers from landing within its borders. Locals claimed it was to protect vineyards from alien interference. Whether tongue-in-cheek or not, the law was real.

807. In July 1807, Napoleon Bonaparte organized a grand rabbit hunt for himself and his men. But instead of fleeing, the released rabbits bizarrely turned and charged at the group, overwhelming them in a surreal and humiliating attack. Despite all of Napoleon's military conquests, it's likely he never lived down being bested by bunnies.

808. Fewer than 120 pilots ever flew the Concorde, the world's first supersonic passenger jet. By comparison, more people have traveled into space. Joining that cockpit club was rarer than becoming an astronaut.

809. In 1800, King George III survived not one, but 2 assassination attempts in a single day. First, a man tried to stab him during a stroll in the park. Later that evening, another would-be assassin fired a pistol at

him inside a crowded theater. Unshaken, the king kept his composure — and famously told the actors to carry on with the show.

810. Between 1898 and 1910, heroin was legally marketed as a cough suppressant by pharmaceutical companies. People were told to take it for colds, not knowing they'd likely become addicted.

811. While Egyptians were building pyramids, woolly mammoths still roamed Wrangel Island off the Siberian coast. These Ice Age giants survived there until around 1650 BCE. Civilizations rose while prehistory quietly held on.

812. Before the French Revolution, which lasted from 1789 to 1799 and turned the guillotine into a symbol, the wool town of Halifax was already dropping a blade in the name of order. Under the "Gibbet Law," anyone caught stealing goods like cloth or livestock could be hauled to a wooden scaffold where a weighted axe sat poised between uprights. A rope held the blade aloft; when cut, gravity did the rest. The device was crude by later standards — no angled edge, no lunette — but it was fast, public, and meant to warn thieves that commerce would be protected at any cost.

The idea gained momentum. By the mid-1500s, Scotland introduced its own refinement, the "Maiden," a cleaner, more engineered version of the Halifax frame. Legend even claims a powerful regent who favored the device eventually met it himself, a grim endorsement from the top. Only much later did France standardize a sleeker, more humane mechanism and give it a notorious name. Long before Paris perfected the drop, Britain had already learned how to let a blade speak for the law.

813. Arthur Priest, a stoker deep in the boiler rooms of ships, earned a reputation as practically unsinkable. He survived the RMS *Olympic's* collision, the *Titanic's* infamous sinking, and even went on to live through multiple wartime disasters — including the sinking of the *Britannic*.

814. After the death of Israel's first president in 1952, the country offered the presidency to Albert Einstein. Though he was honored, Einstein declined, stating he lacked the "natural aptitude" to deal with people. Born in Germany and a theoretical physicist by trade, Einstein knew politics wasn't his calling — even if he was admired worldwide.

815. In 17th-century Arakan, one king chose his wives using a "sniff test" — literally. He smelled sweat-soaked garments to judge a woman's scent before making his selection. If the aroma didn't pass, neither did she.

816. In 2003, Chinese astronaut Yang Liwei heard knocking sounds from outside his spacecraft. The noise couldn't be replicated after landing, but it was later attributed to temperature and pressure changes causing the capsule walls to contract.

817. In 1846, a group of pioneers known as the Donner Party set out for California, lured westward by promises of fertile land and a new life. But after taking an untested shortcut through the mountains, they became trapped by brutal winter snowstorms in the Sierra Nevada. As supplies ran out and rescue efforts stalled, starvation and exposure claimed dozens of lives.

In desperation, survivors resorted to cannibalism, consuming the bodies of those who had died to stay alive. By the time rescuers finally reached them in early 1847, only 48 of the original 87 pioneers remained. The Donner Party's ordeal became one of the most infamous tragedies of westward expansion — a haunting story of ambition, miscalculation, and survival at any cost.

818. Roughly one in every 200 men alive today may carry Y-chromosome DNA linked to Genghis Khan. His empire spread by force, and so did his genes. Centuries later, conquest still echoes in bloodlines.

819. The Nazis revived the guillotine as a tool of terror, installing around 20 in German prisons. Roughly 16,500 people — many of them political prisoners — were executed under its blade. Not all tyranny wore boots; some came with a falling steel edge.

820. In 1510, a group of rats was formally summoned to court in France for destroying a barley crop. Their appointed lawyer claimed they feared for their lives due to neighborhood cats. The judge, surprisingly sympathetic, postponed the trial indefinitely.

821. In 2017, researchers scanned a 1,000-year-old Chinese Buddha statue and made a startling discovery — a mummified monk hidden inside. His organs had been removed, suggesting he had undergone self-

mummification, a rare and excruciating ritual of spiritual devotion. What looked like a simple relic turned out to be a sacred tomb, preserving both body and belief.

822. Cleopatra stuck to tradition and married both her younger brothers — because in ancient Egypt, queens weren't supposed to rule alone. One brother drowned during their messy power struggle, and the other probably ended up poisoned. For Cleopatra, family and politics were a dangerous mix — and being queen meant playing a deadly game where even your own siblings weren't safe.

823. In 1866, Liechtenstein sent 80 soldiers to support Austria in the Austro-Prussian War. Not only did none of them die, but 81 men returned — they'd made a friend along the way. The country disbanded its army shortly after.

824. Tsutomu Yamaguchi was in Hiroshima on August 6, 1945, during the atomic bomb blast. He survived, traveled home to Nagasaki, and was there when the second bomb dropped on August 9. Miraculously, he survived both explosions and lived until 2010. Whether he was the unluckiest or luckiest man alive is up for debate.

825. Florence Nightingale practiced her nursing skills on wounded pets long before tending to soldiers. She kept owls and dozens of cats, and believed that small animals brought comfort to the sick. For her, compassion was both medicine and method.

826. In the 13th century, Pope Gregory IX associated cats — particularly black ones — with devil worship and ordered mass exterminations. Some historians believe this decision worsened the bubonic plague centuries later, as fewer cats meant more rats and more fleas to spread the disease. Others argue the plague spread too rapidly for rats to be the sole cause.

827. In 1932, the Australian military launched a campaign against emus that were damaging crops. Despite using soldiers and machine guns, the birds proved too fast and elusive. The emus won, and the fiasco became known as the "Great Emu War."

828. When Stalin's son Yakov was captured by the Nazis during World War 2, Hitler offered to exchange him for a German officer. Stalin

refused, reportedly declaring, "I will not trade a marshal for a lieutenant," or in some versions, "He is no different from any other Soviet soldier." Yakov later died in a German prison camp.

829. The first British officer killed in World War 1 was an Englishman, born in India, serving in a Scottish regiment, and commanding Senegalese troops in German Togoland. His death stitched together 4 continents under the shadow of one empire.

830. At some point in history, Britain has invaded or fought in 171 out of today's 193 U.N. member states — that's about 90% of the world. The sun may have set on the British Empire, but its military footprints are still stamped across nearly every continent.

831. In the 1890s, Octavia Hatcher of Kentucky was buried after falling into a coma. When her grave was later reopened, signs suggested that she had awakened underground — her nails were bloody and her coffin was scratched.

832. France's Black colonial troops in World War 1 were often sent where survival was least likely. They faced suicide charges and brutal front-line assignments. Their casualty rate was roughly triple that of white soldiers.

833. In 1913, Vienna was quietly hosting a lineup of future giants — and tyrants. For a brief moment, Adolf Hitler, Joseph Stalin, Leon Trotsky, and Josip Broz Tito all lived in the city at the same time, wandering its streets and cafés as unknown men. No one could've guessed that history was percolating in those unassuming coffeehouses.

834. The Weiyang Palace, built during the Han Dynasty in China, once spanned an enormous 1,200 acres (485 hectares), making it far larger than the later Forbidden City in Beijing. It served as the political and ceremonial center of the Han Empire. Despite its former grandeur, almost nothing of the palace remains today — its vast legacy reduced to faint traces in the earth.

835. During World War 1, President Woodrow Wilson let sheep graze the White House lawn to cut maintenance costs. Their wool was auctioned to raise money for the Red Cross. It was wartime thrift with a touch of pastoral politics.

836. In 1962, a strange outbreak of contagious laughter swept through schools in Tanzania. Students laughed uncontrollably for hours, sometimes days, and dozens of schools shut down. It wasn't joy — it was a mass stress response with no clear cure.

837. Nikolai Krasnogorski, a student of famed physiologist Ivan Pavlov, brought his mentor's conditioning experiments from dogs to children — with chilling precision. In the early 20th century, Krasnogorski used orphans as test subjects, surgically implanting metal devices in their mouths to measure salivation just as Pavlov had done with animals. He studied their reflexes to sounds, lights, and other stimuli, attempting to map the mechanics of learning and behavior.

Though his work contributed to the foundations of behavioral science, it also revealed the ethical void of early psychology. These experiments treated vulnerable children as data points, exposing them to invasive procedures without consent.

838. In the late 1880s, an unidentified young woman's body was pulled from the River Seine in Paris. Her serene expression captivated a morgue pathologist, who made a plaster death mask of her face. Dubbed "L'Inconnue de la Seine," her face became a haunting art object and cultural icon. Later, this mask was used as the model for CPR training mannequins around the world — meaning millions have unknowingly practiced mouth-to-mouth on the likeness of a mysterious drowned girl.

839. The oldest still-operating McDonald's, built in 1953 in Downey, California, stayed true to the original McDonald brothers' retro design — resisting Ray Kroc's corporate model for years. It wasn't until 1990 that McDonald's finally took ownership. Today, it stands as a neon-lit time capsule of fast-food history.

840. People living through England's 15th-century civil wars didn't call them the "Wars of the Roses." To contemporaries, they were bitter, rolling struggles between royal cousins — often labeled "the Cousins' War" — as rival branches of the Plantagenets fought, married, and betrayed their way toward the throne. Roses did exist as badges (white for York, red for Lancaster), but they weren't the neat, two-color brand we picture today.

That emblematic framing took shape centuries later. After the Tudors fused the symbols into the red-and-white Tudor rose, Victorian writers romanticized the past, and Sir Walter Scott's 1829 novel *Anne of Geierstein* helped cement the "Wars of the Roses" in the popular imagination. What began as dynastic feuds became a story told in florals — history retrofitted with a tidy name long after the blood had dried.

841. In 1941, Nazi official Rudolf Hess stunned the world by flying solo to Scotland on an unauthorized mission to negotiate peace with Britain. Instead of diplomacy, he got handcuffs — and became the Tower of London's last official state prisoner. His bizarre flight marked one of World War 2's most unexpected twists.

842. Death by elephant was a real form of capital punishment in South and Southeast Asia, especially up to the 19th century. Elephants could be trained to crush bones slowly, toss people, or even use bladed tusks to execute prisoners. While culturally significant at the time, it seems brutally bizarre by modern standards.

15. Substances, Trips & Party Chaos

Alcohol, drugs, and experimental substances shape behavior in wild, unpredictable ways. Behind every party, ritual, or buzz lies a story of risk, change, and occasional disaster.

843. Recent research shows that roughly one-third of suicides involve alcohol or drugs at the time of death, and individuals with substance use disorders face a significantly higher risk of dying by suicide. In the realm of violent crime, alcohol is implicated in about 40% of all violent offenses, including a notably high incidence in sexual assaults and aggravated assaults.

844. Rimonabant was a drug sold in Europe between 2006 and 2008 that suppressed appetite and was considered the "anti-weed." Unlike marijuana, it caused severe depression and was linked to suicides. Though banned, it's still available on the black market.

845. Prolonged use of drugs and alcohol alters the brain's chemistry, particularly in areas related to reward, decision-making, and impulse control. These changes make it extremely difficult to quit through willpower alone, often requiring medical support, therapy, or structured rehabilitation.

846. Ethanol, the active ingredient in alcoholic beverages, is classified as a depressant because it slows down the central nervous system, which can impair judgment, coordination, and reaction time — even in small amounts.

847. The human body is never completely alcohol-free. Tiny amounts are constantly produced in the gut as microbes break down food through fermentation. While the levels are too low to cause intoxication, this natural process means we're all making a little alcohol around the clock.

848. Winston Churchill's drinking habits became almost as famous as his speeches. He was known to start the day with a glass of whiskey, keep brandy close at hand through the afternoon, and wind down with martinis at night. His remarkable tolerance only added to his larger-than-life reputation.

849. Withdrawal from certain substances — particularly alcohol and benzodiazepines — can be dangerous and potentially fatal, with symptoms including seizures and delirium tremens. Medical supervision is essential during detoxification from these substances.

850. Beer lovers can skip the pint glass and grab a spoon instead. Breweries and creameries around the world have crafted beer-flavored ice creams that actually contain alcohol, sometimes up to 5% alcohol by volume. It tastes like dessert, but eat enough scoops and you'll start to feel the buzz.

851. It takes just 6 minutes for alcohol to affect the brain. Even one drink can trigger measurable changes in activity.

852. before breweries and pint glasses, early humans were already experimenting with booze. At Israel's Raqefet Cave, archaeologists found traces of a grain-based, porridge-like beer dating back about 13,000 years. This ancient brew was likely whipped up for ritual feasts by Natufian hunter-gatherers, making it the oldest known evidence of beer-making in the world.

853. Alcohol really can change how we see people, and not just because of lowered inhibitions. Studies suggest drinking dulls the brain's sensitivity to subtle details like facial asymmetry, which normally plays a big role in how we judge attractiveness. The result is the classic "beer goggles" effect, where others may look more appealing than they would sober.

854. Bees aren't immune to alcohol — nectar that ferments in the sun can leave them tipsy. When they stumble back to the hive, other bees often act like strict bouncers, punishing the drunk with bites, shoves, or even forcing them out. Some reports even suggest severe cases end with legs being chewed off to keep them from returning.

855. Vodka has long been Russia's signature spirit, and one practical reason is its resistance to freezing in harsh winters. A standard 80-proof bottle won't solidify until temperatures drop to about minus 17 degrees Fahrenheit (minus 27 degrees Celsius). That makes it both a cultural staple and a reliable drink in subzero climates.

856. In the 1980s and 1990s, U.S. medicine shifted dramatically in its approach to pain. For decades, doctors were cautious with opioids, but pharmaceutical companies aggressively marketed them as safe, advocacy groups pushed for better pain care, and pain was labeled the "fifth vital sign." Physicians began prescribing opioids widely, and between 1999 and 2016, prescription sales nearly quadrupled — as did overdose deaths. Communities became saturated with powerful painkillers, sparking a wave of dependence that devastated families and drove many users to heroin and fentanyl when prescriptions dried up.

What began as a well-meaning reform turned into one of the deadliest public health crises in U.S. history. Lawsuits later revealed how drug companies misled doctors and regulators, while a lack of oversight allowed the epidemic to spread unchecked.

857. A 2023 study found that an estimated 40% to 60% of domestic violence cases involve alcohol or drug use, with substances often acting as triggers or intensifiers rather than root causes. Alcohol lowers inhibitions and increases aggression, while drugs can impair emotional control — making violent episodes more frequent or severe.

858. New Zealand once experimented with an alcohol-free bar, hoping to attract people looking for a sober night out. But with drinks priced around $15 for a little more than fancy water, customers quickly lost interest. The bar shut its doors in just five weeks, proving the concept a tough sell.

859. Alcohol is the most commonly abused substance in the U.S. Roughly 25.8% of adults aged 18 and older report binge drinking in a 4-month period. Also, alcohol is linked to approximately 95,000 deaths annually, making it the third-leading preventable cause of death in the U.S. In 2019, 28% of all driving fatalities were alcohol-related.

860. Some U.S. states still maintain "dry counties" where alcohol sales are banned. These laws date back to Prohibition.

861. Adults over 65 are among the largest groups misusing prescription drugs. In 2013 alone, 55 million opioid and 28.4 million depressant prescriptions were written for seniors, with misuse among this group more than doubling between 2002 and 2012.

862. A teenage girl started drinking alcohol after reading online that it could help with weight loss, which led to addiction and eventually influenced her friends to start drinking too.

863. Roughly 28% of college dropouts report struggling with alcohol abuse, suggesting a troubling link between substance misuse and academic failure. The connection is complicated: stress, financial pressure, social environments, and untreated mental health issues often overlap, creating a cycle where drinking and poor performance feed into one another.

While alcohol abuse doesn't explain every dropout case, the statistic highlights how deeply substance use can shape a student's future. Behind the numbers are stories of overwhelmed young adults navigating high expectations and newfound independence — and how those pressures can quietly derail even the most promising paths.

864. A 2025 study by American Addiction Centers found that 15.3% of U.S. workers admitted to being under the influence of alcohol on the job, while 2.9% reported using illicit drugs at work — behaviors strongly tied to reduced productivity, higher absenteeism, workplace accidents, and increased turnover.

865. Substance dependency is a medically treatable condition that can be managed through a combination of therapies, including behavioral counseling, medications, physical activity, and peer support. Successful recovery often involves a personalized, long-term approach that addresses both physical dependence and underlying psychological or social factors.

866. Beer isn't just popular — it's one of the most widely consumed drinks on the planet. Alongside staples like water and tea, it consistently ranks at the very top of global beverage consumption. Its long history and cultural significance help explain why it remains such a worldwide favorite.

867. Commonly abused prescription drugs include opioids like hydrocodone, oxycodone, and codeine. These medications are often taken in higher doses than prescribed — or by people who didn't get the prescription in the first place.

868. A champagne bottle is under serious pressure — around 90 PSI, which is roughly three times the pressure in a car tire. That force is what

makes the cork fly with such speed, but it also means mishandling can cause injuries. It's part of the thrill of the pop, but also a good reason to aim carefully.

869. People with blue eyes may be more prone to alcohol dependence. Studies suggest they have lower alcohol tolerance than those with darker eyes.

870. As of 2015, an estimated 100 million Americans suffer from chronic pain, leading to widespread and sometimes excessive prescriptions of painkillers and antidepressants.

871. In the 1800s, American children were taught extreme myths about alcohol. They were told a single sip could make them blind, insane, or even burst into flames.

872. In the U.K., drinking is woven into daily life on a staggering scale. Every single second, people collectively down about 247 pints of beer and 232 glasses of wine. It's a snapshot of just how central alcohol is to British social culture.

873. In Russia, one controversial treatment for alcoholism involves surgically implanting a capsule under the skin that slowly releases disulfiram, a drug used to deter drinking. If the person consumes alcohol, the medication causes severe withdrawal-like reactions such as nausea, vomiting, and dizziness. The intense discomfort is meant to create a strong aversion to alcohol, though the method is debated among medical professionals.

874. Marijuana, cocaine, and hallucinogens are the most widely used illegal drugs.

875. Over the course of a lifetime, the average Brit is estimated to spend about £50,000 (roughly $62,000) on alcohol. That adds up to quite a tab for pints, cocktails, and wine over the years.

876. A 2024 study reports that many adolescents begin experimenting with substances early in their teens. Studies show average initiation ages of about 13 for alcohol, with drug experimentation generally occurring between ages 13 and 15.

877. Relapse occurs in 40% to 60% of people recovering from addiction, a rate comparable to chronic illnesses like asthma or diabetes.

878. Ecstasy, or MDMA, was originally developed in a lab setting but was later adopted by rave culture in the 1980s. By 2014, it had caused over 45 deaths in the U.K. and had become one of the top illegal recreational drugs.

879. All standard alcoholic drinks contain roughly the same amount of ethanol, so consuming wine or beer will get you just as intoxicated as an equal amount of hard liquor.

880. In 2018, a bottle of vodka valued at $1.25 million was stolen from a Copenhagen bar, making headlines as the world's priciest vodka. Days later, police recovered it at a construction site — emptied of its contents. Whether the thieves drank it or just ditched it remains a mystery.

881. A speedball is a risky drug combination of cocaine, a stimulant, and heroin, a depressant. The opposing effects can create a deceptive sense of control or heightened tolerance, as the sedation masks the stimulant's strain and vice versa, significantly increasing the risk of overdose, making speedballs especially lethal.

882. Long before vodka became a social drink, it was used medicinally in Europe centuries ago. Doctors prescribed it for ailments ranging from infections to fatigue.

883. Teenagers are especially vulnerable to addiction because their brains are still developing. Early drug use increases the risk of long-term dependency by approximately 40%, and some high schoolers report using dangerous substances such as methamphetamines.

884. Recovery can begin at any stage of substance use, and early intervention increases the chances of success.

885. Prescription painkillers cause approximately 50 deaths per day in the U.S. and now lead to more fatalities than heroin and cocaine combined.

886. Addiction rewires the brain's reward system. Drugs and compulsive behaviors trigger surges of dopamine so large that everyday pleasures start to feel muted by comparison. Over time, the circuitry that steers judg-

ment, memory, and impulse control is dragged into the loop; the result is a brain that learns to seek the substance first and everything else second, even when the costs are obvious. That learning isn't a moral failing — it's biology doing what it does best: adapting, then getting stuck.

From the outside, this can be hard to see. Many people with substance problems are highly functional: they hold jobs, keep families together, and look "fine" until the cracks widen. Addiction cuts across profession, education, income, and status; it doesn't care how successful someone appears.

The costs are enormous, measured in more than pain. In the U.S., addiction drains hundreds of billions of dollars each year through healthcare, lost productivity, and crime. Yet treatment pays society back: for every dollar invested, several are saved down the line as hospitalizations, arrests, and workplace losses fall. Recovery is difficult because the brain has been changed — but it's not impossible.

887. Australian scientists created a hangover-free beer by adding electrolytes. The lighter version was found to be three times more hydrating than regular beer.

888. Freon, a gas found in refrigerators and air conditioners, can be inhaled to get high. Side effects include hallucinations, heart problems, lung damage, coma, and even death. It's nicknamed "the Breath of Death."

889. Prescription drug addiction is expected to remain a major issue for future generations, prompting policy changes and increased regulation. In 2015, President Obama launched a national initiative to combat opioid abuse, which included funding for treatment programs, stricter prescription guidelines, and increased awareness campaigns.

890. Zolpidem, a prescription sleep aid, can lead to seizures, addiction, and death. It has been misused as a date rape drug and is known to cause sleepwalking and even sleep-driving, sometimes resulting in fatal accidents.

891. Until 2013, beer wasn't legally considered alcohol in Russia. It was sold everywhere like soda until a new law reclassified it.

892. Police were called to a raucous house party in Maryland in 2017, expecting the usual: loud music, red cups, and a sea of students. What they didn't expect was for the very air to register on a breathalyzer. When officers tested the atmosphere inside, the device flashed positive for alcohol vapor — a sign of just how much booze had been opened, spilled, and aerosolized in the packed rooms.

Inside, students were scattered across sticky floors and crowded hallways, many underage, the house humid with the smell of beer and grain alcohol. Officers began clearing the place, handing out citations and calling parents as the party's legend wrote itself in real time. It wasn't just a bust; it was a cautionary tale that sounded like an urban myth — a gathering so soaked in alcohol that even the air was technically drunk.

893. Most hard liquors — like gin, whiskey, and vodka — are vegan-friendly. Cream-based spirits, like Baileys, are the exception.

894. A 2023 study published in *JAMA Network Open* analyzed data from over 150,000 men and found that excessive alcohol consumption — especially more than 14 drinks per week — was linked to a significantly higher risk of premature death. The study highlighted increased mortality from causes such as liver disease, cancer, and heart conditions, reinforcing public health guidelines on limiting alcohol intake.

895. "Wet" is a street drug made by combining marijuana with PCP, a powerful hallucinogenic drug also known as phencyclidine. It causes dissociation and hallucinations, and has been linked to violent crimes, including the murder of children by users under its influence.

896. A 2024 study reported that roughly 56% of injured roadway users tested positive for alcohol, THC, or other substances.

897. I-dosing is a method of inducing altered mental states using specific sound frequencies through headphones. It can simulate drug-like experiences such as euphoria or anxiety and is available for free online, including on YouTube.

898. Carbogen is a gas mixture of 70% oxygen and 30% carbon dioxide that creates a suffocating sensation when inhaled. It can trigger the brain

to release DMT, a powerful naturally occurring psychedelic, producing a hallucinogenic high often accompanied by intense fear.

899. A small number of people live with oenophobia — an intense fear of wine. Just being near a bottle can spark feelings of panic or anxiety, even though for most, wine in moderation is perfectly harmless. Like other phobias, it's less about the object itself and more about the emotional response it provokes.

900. The custom of making a "toast" goes all the way back to ancient Rome. Back then, people would drop a piece of charred or spiced bread into wine to soften its acidity and improve the taste. Over time, the practice shifted from flavoring the drink to raising a glass in celebration.

901. Around 1 in 4 people seem to be naturally resistant to hangovers. No matter how much they drink, they rarely wake up with the pounding headache or nausea that others dread. Scientists aren't sure why, but genetics and metabolism may give these lucky few a free pass.

902. Opioids are driving a major public health crisis in the U.S., with over 80,000 overdose deaths reported in 2023 — an increase of 300% since 2016. Fentanyl, a synthetic opioid 50 times more potent than heroin, is present in an estimated 70% of illicit drugs.

16. Atrocities, Brutality & Dark Warfare

Whether through secret drugs, inventive torture devices, or mass atrocities on the battlefield, war has produced shocking methods of control, suffering, and survival that defy belief.

903. In 1954, the U.S. military detonated Castle Bravo, its most powerful hydrogen bomb, at Bikini Atoll in the Marshall Islands. The blast was far stronger than predicted, sending radioactive fallout across inhabited atolls. Islanders developed radiation burns, nausea, and hair loss within days. Though residents were evacuated, many were later studied without informed consent under Project 4.1, which tracked the effects of radiation exposure on humans.

For decades, Marshallese communities suffered high rates of thyroid disease, miscarriages, and birth defects, while some were resettled on islands still dangerously contaminated. The tests left lasting scars: poisoned land, cultural upheaval, and generations of health problems.

904. The breaking wheel, also called the Catherine wheel, was an ancient Greek invention widely used in medieval Europe for public execution. Victims were tied to a large wooden wheel, and their limbs were systematically broken before being hoisted on a stake to die. Other variations included rolling victims downhill or suspending them over flames, burning them alive.

905. In World War 1, Canadian troops became known for their relentless style. They raided trenches with speed and aggression, often pushing deeper into enemy lines than expected. Shock tactics and quick improvisation gave them an edge, and wherever they fought, the quiet "Live and Let Live" understandings that sometimes softened the front tended to vanish. For the Canadians, war was something to press, not to pause.

906. In ancient Rome, the condemned were sometimes tossed into the arena unarmed against lions, tigers, or bears — not to fight, but to die. Denied even the dignity of combat, they became living symbols in a spectacle of fear. The blood and terror entertained the crowds while also

sending a message: Rome's power was absolute, mercy was scarce, and escape was impossible.

907. In March and April 1945, several U.S. units adopted informal "take no prisoners" orders, motivated by the discovery of Nazi atrocities and the ongoing resistance of German troops. Historian Stephen Ambrose reported that one-third of the 1,000 interviewed veterans had seen executions of surrendering Germans.

908. In the summer of 1943, the Eastern Front became a furnace. Hitler launched Operation Citadel at Kursk, aiming to pinch off a vast Soviet salient with a double-pronged assault. What the Wehrmacht met instead were layered defenses — belts of trenches and anti-tank ditches, webs of barbed wire, and some of the densest minefields ever laid. Artillery rolled like thunder across open farmland; Stukas screamed; infantry clawed forward yard by yard. At Prokhorovka on July 12, hundreds of tanks crashed together at knife-fight range, turning fields into scrap and soil into blackened glass.

The offensive stalled, then snapped. As news of the Allied landing in Sicily forced Hitler to call off Citadel, the Red Army counterattacked at Orel and Kharkov, grinding the Germans backward. In roughly 50 days, casualties mounted into the hundreds of thousands, and the wreckage — burned hulls, torn tracks, shattered guns — littered the steppe for miles. Kursk didn't just end a battle; it ended Germany's ability to choose the terms of the war in the East. From that point on, the initiative belonged to the Soviets, and the road west was paved with the ruins left behind.

909. Modern war isn't supposed to be a free-for-all. Treaties like the Hague and Geneva Conventions lay down rules meant to reduce suffering, protecting civilians, medics, prisoners of war, cultural treasures, and even things like water and power plants. Homes, schools, hospitals, and museums are all shielded — unless someone turns them into military targets, at which point the protection falls away.

910. Faking surrender, feigning injury, or misusing protected symbols such as the red cross or neutral flags to deceive the enemy is considered perfidy and constitutes a war crime.

911. During the 2008 to 2009 Gaza conflict, white phosphorus munitions were deployed over densely populated neighborhoods, burning at extreme temperatures and adhering to skin. Hospitals, schools, and U.N. facilities were struck, resulting in deep, recurring chemical burns and widespread fires. In some cases, victims reignited when embedded particles were exposed to air. Human rights organizations alleged unlawful use near civilians, despite military claims that the munitions were intended solely for smoke screens.

912. The use of child soldiers is prohibited, and under international law, individuals who were under 18 at the time of the alleged offense cannot be sentenced to death.

913. Flaying alive involved carefully removing a victim's skin while keeping them alive. Executioners often "softened" victims first with sunburn or boiling water to make skin removal easier. Skilled torturers could keep victims alive for days, with death usually caused by blood loss, infection, or hypothermia from lack of skin.

914. The Iron Maiden was a spiked coffin designed to trap a victim upright and pierce their body without killing them immediately, causing extended agony. Though some historians question its existence, it's often depicted as a medieval torture device that inflicted slow suffering.

915. At Abu Ghraib prison from 2003 to 2004, detainees were stripped, stacked, terrorized with dogs, and abused while U.S. personnel photographed the scenes. An internal investigation called the abuse systemic, not spontaneous. Many prisoners had never been charged with crimes. Lower-ranking guards were punished, but high-level accountability largely failed.

916. Japan's wartime "comfort stations" coerced or kidnapped tens of thousands of women from occupied regions to serve soldiers. Many were teenagers, transported under false job promises, and forced to "service" dozens daily. Beatings, disease, and deaths were common; survivors often faced lifelong stigma. Official recognition and redress have remained partial and contested.

917. "The rack" worked by ropes and cranks that slowly stretched the body, pulling joints out of place and tearing muscles with each turn. It

wasn't about truth so much as submission — confessions came whether or not someone was guilty. The drawn-out pace was deliberate, making pain itself the tool to shatter resistance and force obedience.

918. The Blood Eagle, a legendary Norse execution method, involved cutting a person's back, breaking their ribs, and pulling out their lungs to create "wings." Though described in sagas written during the 12th and 13th centuries and attributed to events in the Viking Age, which spanned roughly from 793 to 1066 CE, there is no archaeological evidence that it was actually practiced. Most historians believe victims would have died quickly from the initial wounds, and some argue the ritual may have been a literary invention or a mistranslation of poetic metaphors.

919. The Soviet "Dead Hand" (or Perimeter) system was designed to launch a retaliatory nuclear strike automatically if leadership and communications were destroyed. Sensors, algorithms, and command rockets could issue launch orders even after a decapitation attack. Its purpose was to guarantee mutual annihilation, not to prevent it. Public details of its current status are scarce, by design.

920. During the Cold War, which lasted from 1945 to 1991, bioweapons programs developed deadly agents like anthrax, plague, and even modified smallpox, and today's gene-editing tools have made creating dangerous pathogens easier than ever.

921. Under King Leopold II's private rule of the Congo Free State, which lasted from 1885 to 1908, brutal rubber quotas were enforced through hostage-taking, public whippings with the chicotte, and systematic mutilation. Soldiers were ordered to cut off victims' hands as proof of bullets used, turning severed hands into a grim form of currency.

922. The Swedish Drink was a method used during the Thirty Years' War, which lasted from 1618 to 1648, where victims were force-fed a mixture of feces and urine until their stomachs were painfully bloated. Torturers sometimes applied pressure with boards or sticks to cause vomiting or internal injuries. It was designed to humiliate as well as torture.

923. The Rif War between Spain and Berber tribes in northern Morocco from 1921 to 1926 saw atrocities committed by both sides. In one incident, Rif fighters killed 2,000 surrendering Spanish soldiers. In retalia-

tion, Spain conducted chemical attacks with mustard gas and chloropicrin on civilian populations, contaminating markets and rivers, leaving a legacy of illness and cancer in the region.

924. Oubliettes, or "forgotten" dungeons, were narrow underground cells where prisoners were left to die of starvation or dehydration, often among rotting corpses and rats. Some were kept alive for years with minimal food and water, hearing life outside but never experiencing it again. Discoveries in castles like Leap Castle in Ireland revealed oubliettes filled with hundreds of skeletons, showing they were rarely cleaned.

925. Gibbeting involved locking prisoners in tight iron cages, hoisting them high in public, and leaving them to die and decompose as a warning. The smell of rotting bodies often tormented nearby towns for years, with some remains left for decades before being removed.

926. After liberating Dachau concentration camp on April 29, 1945, U.S. troops from the 157th Infantry Regiment shot and killed surrendered SS guards, with one famous photograph showing 16 men lined up before being killed. Eyewitnesses reported U.S. soldiers executing guards in train cars and towers, while camp survivors, under American supervision, beat and stomped others to death. General Patton ordered an investigation, but it was suppressed until 1991, and no one was charged.

927. Inside Nazi concentration camps, physicians turned medicine into torture. Prisoners — including children and twins — were subjected to experiments without anesthesia or consent, their suffering logged with clinical precision. Victims were deliberately infected with deadly diseases, submerged in freezing water to test survival limits, crushed in pressure chambers, or sterilized in attempts to advance Nazi eugenics. Many were dissected immediately after death so data could be harvested.

Doctors like Josef Mengele framed these atrocities as "research," but their meticulous records revealed systematic brutality, not science. When the camps were liberated, the world was horrified by the scale of medical crimes committed in the name of progress. The Nuremberg Trial, held from 1945 to 1946, exposed these experiments and led to the creation of the Nuremberg Code in 1947, establishing principles like informed consent — basic ethics that the perpetrators had completely ignored.

928. Following a contested coup attempt in Indonesia in 1965, the army and allied militias carried out mass killings of alleged communists and sympathizers. Accusations often required no evidence, and rivers in Java ran with bodies, while tens of thousands were slaughtered in Bali.

929. The Spanish Tickler was a handheld claw-like torture device, similar to metal talons, used to shred flesh from victims' bodies. It was applied slowly and methodically, sometimes down to the bone, and survivors often died from infection. Although brutal, historians debate whether it was widely used.

930. Medical personnel, facilities, vehicles, and evacuation points marked with recognized emblems, such as a red cross on a white background, are protected; deliberately targeting them is a war crime.

931. Waterboarding restrains a person on an incline, covers the face with a cloth, and pours water over it to trigger the sensation of drowning. It was prized historically because it leaves few outward marks while producing extreme panic and compliance. Earlier forms sometimes omitted the cloth or forced massive water intake, leading to drowning or stomach rupture.

932. The "Judas cradle," also called the Judas chair, was a medieval torture device that forced a naked prisoner to sit on a sharp, pyramid-shaped seat. Interrogators could add weights or adjust pressure, causing severe tearing, bleeding, and internal injuries, often leading to fatal infections. Victims were sometimes left on the device for hours or days, with intermittent pressure cycles designed to maximize pain and psychological torment.

933. The Bengal famine of 1943 wasn't just a natural disaster but a man-made tragedy. Triggered by a cyclone and crop failures, the crisis was worsened by British colonial policies that diverted food supplies, seized rice for the war effort, and imposed "denial" measures to keep resources from falling into Japanese hands. Grain prices soared beyond reach, and imports that might have eased the famine never came.

As millions starved, trains and city streets filled with the dying, while shipments of food moved elsewhere. Relief arrived late and proved inadequate, and by the time it ended, an estimated 2 to 3 million people were dead. The famine became one of the darkest chapters of British rule in India, illustrating how wartime priorities and indifference magnified suffering on a staggering scale.

934. To count as lawful combatants, soldiers have to wear uniforms or at least a clear, fixed sign that can be seen from a distance. This requirement is part of international humanitarian law and helps distinguish fighters from civilians. Anyone fighting in civilian clothes risks being treated as a spy, and if they're caught, they can lose the protections normally given to prisoners of war.

935. Judicial sawing ranged from amputating a thief's finger or hand to the extreme case of bisecting a person. In the worst form, the victim was hung upside down and sawn from the groin toward the head with a two-man saw. Death came relatively quickly from blood loss and shock — unless executioners deliberately slowed the process. This gruesome punishment was carried out publicly in regions such as medieval Europe, the Ottoman Empire, and Edo-period Japan, often in marketplaces or execution grounds, to serve as a stark warning to would-be offenders and reinforce state authority through fear.

936. Combat medics are allowed to carry small arms, but only to protect themselves and the wounded in their care. The moment they switch to offensive fighting, they lose their special protection under the rules of war.

937. On April 19, 1945, U.S. troops executed a group of captured 14-year-old Hitler Youth trainees in Treseburg after suffering heavy losses in battle, including the alleged killing of a commander by a sniper disguised in civilian clothes. A survivor later testified to the murders, and exhumations conducted in 1951 confirmed the boys had been shot in the back of the neck.

938. During World War 1, German troops invaded Belgium and committed systematic atrocities against civilians. With fears of Belgian guerrilla fighters, they burned villages, executed civilians, and even assaulted nuns under the pretense of searching for disguised men. The Germans also destroyed Leuven University's library, burning 230,000 books and nearly 1,000 manuscripts in an effort to erase Belgian culture.

939. In medieval London, there was a dungeon in the Tower of London connected to the river that would fill with rats whenever water levels rose, driving them toward chained prisoners. The rats attacked and bit prisoners repeatedly, often while they slept, leaving them covered in wounds. Some prisoners were left in the dungeon for weeks until they died, and later this method was used as a form of execution where victims were simply abandoned.

940. Bamboo torture allegedly involved tying a victim over young bamboo shoots, which could grow up to 36 inches (91 centimeters) in a single day, eventually piercing through the body and reaching vital organs. Some claims say that this method would cause an agonizingly slow death as the bamboo stalks steadily grew through the victim, though evidence for its historical use is limited.

941. Modern warfare comes with a blunt rulebook: if a weapon either causes superfluous injury or can't be aimed cleanly, it doesn't belong on the battlefield. That's why poisons, chemical agents, and biological agents are out — once released, they don't respect uniforms or borders, and their spread can't be called back. Anti-personnel landmines are treated the same way: their victims are often civilians long after the shooting stops, so where they exist, they must be mapped, marked, and cleared; plastic mines designed to slip past metal detectors are forbidden outright. Lasers designed to cause permanent blindness violate the same legal boundaries, even though targeting lasers used for aiming or communication are still permitted.

Other munitions fail the "needless suffering" test. Expanding or exploding bullets meant to rip open tissue and projectiles that shatter into non-detectable fragments are barred because surgeons can't reliably find and remove what's left behind. Incendiaries like napalm and flamethrowers sit under tight restrictions — never in civilian areas, and only when no less harmful option can do the job. Cluster munitions, with their wide scatter and high dud rates, are banned by many states for leaving behind lethal bomblets that function like landmines for years. The through-line is simple: the law tries to keep combat brutal but bounded, drawing hard lines where weapons either outlast the war or make suffering the point.

942. Lingchi, or "death by a thousand cuts," was a brutal public execution method in imperial China reserved for the most serious crimes, such as treason or parricide. Executioners deliberately made numerous small cuts, carefully avoiding vital organs to prolong agony and consciousness, while opium was sometimes given to dull the pain. Beyond physical torment, the mutilation carried a deep spiritual stigma, as dismemberment was believed to affect one's afterlife. Lingchi could last from minutes to hours, and graphic photographs from the late Qing era fueled outrage and contributed to its abolition in 1905.

943. Archaeological evidence suggests torture was already practiced about 7,000 years ago in early Neolithic Europe, showing that cruelty and torture have been part of human behavior for millennia. While torture is still used in some parts of the world, most Western countries no longer practice it officially.

944. "White torture" uses total sensory monotony — a white cell, white clothes, white food, constant light — to disorient and psychologically break the prisoner. Deprivation and lack of variation can induce anxiety, hallucinations, and severe stress without obvious physical marks. Reports associate it with modern security services and "enhanced interrogation" programs. Its power lies in cumulative duration rather than acute pain.

945. The "tiger bench" is a reported torture method used in parts of China, where a detainee is strapped to a narrow bench with their back and head supported by a board. The feet are then elevated by placing bricks underneath until extreme tension builds in the legs. Victims have reported injuries ranging from torn ligaments to exposed ankle bones.

946. Clergy serving spiritual needs at the front are protected as non-combatants.

947. In August 1945, 2 airburst nuclear bombs — 1 over Hiroshima and 1 over Nagasaki — instantly killed tens of thousands of civilians and incinerated entire districts. Temperatures near ground zero reached thousands of degrees, leaving "shadows" etched into stone and catastrophic burns. Radiation sickness followed, causing hair loss, bleeding, and organ failure for many who initially survived. By the end of 1945, the combined death toll was in the hundreds of thousands.

948. Strappado is a torture method that involves binding a victim's hands behind their back and suspending them by the wrists, which places extreme stress on the shoulders, often leading to dislocations and nerve damage. In some cases, it's combined with beatings, electric shocks, or high-pressure water to intensify the pain. While its origins date back to medieval Europe, modern reports have documented its use in countries such as Turkey, Vietnam, Cambodia, and even in certain U.S. detention contexts.

949. The cat-o'-nine-tails, a multi-tailed whipping device, remains part of judicial punishment in parts of the Caribbean. Reinstated in the 1990s in countries like Antigua and Barbados, some versions use barbed wire or knotted cords. Its use has drawn torture allegations and international criticism, yet it persists under claims of deterrence.

950. References to "modern" psychological techniques also include blasting loud music and combining it with isolation to degrade a prisoner's mental state. The goal is sleep loss, anxiety, and learned helplessness rather than visible injury. Some individuals resist or find specific stimuli less aversive, but the method relies on duration and deprivation. It underscores how contemporary practices can inflict profound harm without overt wounds.

951. The Syrian box method is a form of torture still used by security services during the country's civil conflict. Prisoners are bound inside a small, tilted box that is deliberately too cramped to allow standing, sitting, or lying down. The angle also causes any food or water to slide out of reach. Detainees held in this position are often subjected to electric shocks, compounding the physical and psychological torment. The method is designed to induce exhaustion, helplessness, and long-term trauma.

952. In the Soviet Union, authorities weaponized psychiatry by diagnosing political dissidents with "sluggish schizophrenia" and imprisoning them in psychiatric hospitals. Victims were forcibly drugged with heavy antipsychotics, subjected to electroshock therapy, and kept in isolation to crush resistance. Even after release, the diagnosis ruined their reputations and careers. Global outrage over this abuse of medicine eventually pressured the Soviet Union into limited psychiatric reforms.

953. Armed groups have abducted children and conditioned them into fighters through beatings, drugs, and forced atrocities. Boys carry rifles as tall as themselves; girls are enslaved as "wives" for commanders. The intent is to sever ties to home and normalize violence. Reintegration later is fraught with PTSD, addiction, and community stigma.

954. The ducking stool, developed in the 16th century as a so-called "moral corrective device," was used primarily in England and colonial America on women accused of gossip, witchcraft, or sexual impropriety. The victim would be strapped into the chair and repeatedly submerged in water — sometimes to the point of unconsciousness or death. Far from a simple punishment, the device was a public spectacle designed to humiliate, turning discipline into both ritual and warning.

955. In German Southwest Africa — modern-day Namibia — colonial authorities carried out a genocide against the Herero and Nama peoples between 1904 and 1908, issuing formal extermination orders that led to mass killings and starvation. People were driven into the desert with wells blocked, then confined to lethal camps like Shark Island. Death rates were catastrophic, and bodies were exploited for racial "science." The genocide was the harbinger of later doctrines of racial hierarchy.

956. A medieval torture device known as the iron chair featured between 500 and 1,500 spikes embedded into its surface. Victims were strapped in so the spikes pierced their flesh, sometimes for days, and occasionally a fire was lit beneath the chair to intensify the pain. This brutal method was used in parts of Europe until the late 1800s.

17. Mysterious Rites & Ancient Customs

From ancient Rome to modern cults, rituals and beliefs have shaped societies in strange and sometimes horrifying ways, exposing humanity's fascination with the sacred, the supernatural, and the shocking.

957. Green magic works hand-in-hand with nature, weaving spells from leaves, roots, flowers, and the rhythms of the Earth. It follows the flow of the seasons and moon phases, timing rituals to when the world is most open. Practitioners craft potions, charms, and remedies for healing, protection, fertility, and calm. At its heart, it's about living in balance — with care, with purpose, and with deep respect for the land that gives.

958. At Easter, Greeks paint eggs red to symbolize the blood of Christ. Players tap eggs against each other, and the last uncracked egg is said to bring its holder good luck for the year. While festive and fun, the game carries a deep spiritual symbolism that connects competition with faith.

959. Stories of demons answering "Enns" — short chants such as "Tasa fubin Andromalius onca" — highlight the power of rhythm and repetition in ritual. Repeated invocations can quiet the mind, heighten focus, and build emotional intensity, whether interpreted as summoning a spirit or simply inducing a meditative trance state.

960. The Celts conducted human sacrifices as part of their religious practices. Ancient sources describe victims stabbed for prophecy or burned alive in wicker structures filled with animals and humans. Archaeological evidence, such as the Lindow Man, supports these accounts: his body shows signs of strangulation, a head wound, and a slit throat before burial in a bog.

961. Zoroastrians wear a sacred woolen cord called a kushti, tied around the waist with specific knots. Adherents must untie and retie it in silence several times a day, facing a source of light. For priests, the ritual is even more frequent. The act symbolizes purity, discipline, and constant remembrance of faith. Originating in ancient Persia (modern-day Iran), Zoroastrianism is one of the world's oldest monotheistic religions.

962. In Classic Maya society, sexuality functioned as sacred theater tied to cosmology, kingship, and statecraft; royal couples staged sexual-ritual performances to legitimize power and secure cosmic and agricultural balance.

963. At Teotihuacan, the great "City of the Gods" in Mexico, archaeologists uncovered the Pyramid of the Moon filled with human remains. Among them were children sacrificed in elaborate ceremonies, likely to consecrate the massive monuments. Strangely, the builders left no written records, making the meaning of these rituals one of Mesoamerica's enduring mysteries.

964. The Answer Man requires 10 players with phones. Everyone calls the person to the left. Only one line connects — to him. He answers your question but then asks his own. Refuse or fail, and legend says you'll lose a body part in life soon after, or even feel his gnarled hand take it then and there.

965. Among the Dani tribe of Indonesia, women once cut off the tips of their fingers to express grief after a loved one's death. The act was believed to both manifest mourning physically and ward off vengeful spirits. Though no longer common, evidence of the practice remains visible among older generations.

966. In Bali, adolescents take part in a traditional tooth-filing ceremony that symbolizes the smoothing away of human vices like lust, greed, and pride. During the rite, the upper canines and incisors are gently filed down, marking the transition into adulthood. It's considered an essential ritual, traditionally required before marriage to ensure spiritual balance and social readiness.

967. One of the oldest and most lasting traditions in China is ancestor worship, which has been around for thousands of years. At its heart is the belief that the spirits of the dead remain active within the family, capable of blessing or troubling the living, depending on how they are remembered. Families honor their lineage with offerings of food, incense, and prayers, ensuring that ancestors are cared for in the afterlife and that ties across generations remain unbroken.

One of the most important rituals is Qingming, or Tomb-Sweeping Day, held each spring. Families travel to ancestral graves to clean the tombs, present gifts of fruit, tea, and symbolic paper money, and bow in reverence. It's both solemn and celebratory: a day of remembrance, gratitude, and renewal of family bonds.

Despite centuries of political upheaval and modernization, ancestral worship endures across China and beyond, practiced in both grand temples and humble homes. It's more than ritual — it's a way of seeing life itself as part of a continuous chain, where the living and the dead share a dialogue of memory, duty, and respect.

968. Succubi and incubi — seductive spirits that visit humans in the night — appear across many cultures. Medieval Christian writers warned about them as demonic tempters, while modern interpreters see them as expressions of repressed desire, dreams, or sleep paralysis.

969. Sigils — the unique symbols tied to a specific demon — were believed to be the spirit's "signature." Memorizing or meditating on them worked like a symbolic password, a way of attuning one's mind to a specific archetype or force. Modern chaos magicians reinterpret sigils as psychological tools for focusing intent, rather than literal summoning.

970. In Yoruba tradition, which is practiced in Nigeria, Benin, and the diaspora, Egúngún masquerades represent the living presence of ancestors. Dancers wear towering, layered costumes of fabric and charms, their identities concealed as they move to the beat of drums and chants. Once dressed, the person inside is no longer seen as themselves but as the returned ancestor — a presence treated with reverence, where showing disrespect is taboo.

Every turn, leap, or swirl of cloth is read as communication. Movements and drum rhythms are believed to carry ancestral messages: blessings, warnings, or judgments meant to guide the community. These performances aren't entertainment alone but rituals that preserve harmony, reinforce moral order, and link the living to their lineage.

971. Circles, pentagrams, and candles in rituals weren't just "occult" props but tools of focus. A circle symbolized protection, the cardinal candles represented the 4 elements, and the pentagram was a diagram of the

universe. In psychological terms, they created a powerful "mental container" to help participants shift into a trance-like state.

972. The Incas sacrificed humans, especially children, to appease gods and prevent natural disasters like earthquakes, floods, and volcanic eruptions. Children were considered the purest offerings and were sometimes raised solely for ritual killing. Before sacrifice, they were honored with feasts, fine diets, and even meetings with the emperor, under the belief they would live happily in the afterlife.

973. In India, the Aghori are a tiny, controversial Shaiva sect associated with cremation grounds and taboo-breaking ascetic practices meant to transcend fear and impurity. They're often described as smearing ash from pyres, meditating near corpses, and using bones as ritual objects; sensational claims of cannibalism exist in reportage and folklore but aren't representative of mainstream Hinduism and are disputed or contextualized as transgressive rites.

974. Black mirrors, candles, and incense used for "scrying" weren't necessarily about demons — they were methods of divination. Gazing into reflective surfaces to see visions is found in ancient Greek oracles, Aztec obsidian mirrors, and modern fortune-telling. Psychologists compare this to pareidolia — seeing images in random patterns — heightened by suggestion.

975. Mesopotamians practiced human sacrifice as part of royal burials. Palace attendants, warriors, and handmaidens were killed to accompany rulers into the afterlife, their bodies placed in decorative order with weapons or ornaments. Once thought to have been poisoned, evidence now shows they were killed brutally with a pike through the skull.

976. Necromancy is the art of reaching across the veil to speak with the dead — seeking insight, warnings, or hidden truths. Older rites called for grave soil, bones, or blood, with spirits summoned into mirrors, vessels, or dreams. Medieval texts often painted it as dark or demonic, but in modern hands, it can look more like ancestor veneration or mediumship. Whether it's done with ritual or reverence, the goal is the same: listen to what the dead still know.

977. Sex magic channels sexual energy as a kind of rocket fuel for intention. The moment of orgasm — when focus sharpens and the line between conscious and subconscious blurs — is seen as prime time to launch a goal, charge a sigil, or visualize a desired outcome. It's not just about pleasure; it's about using that surge to shift reality or spark spiritual awakening.

978. Japan's Sokushinbutsu tradition involved years of self-mummification through extreme fasting and meditation, and ending in voluntary entombment. Practiced into the 20th century, it resulted in at least 2 dozen preserved monk bodies that are still displayed in temples today.

979. In demonological lore, Andromalius is portrayed as a guardian against theft or harm, often arriving with a snake — a motif that recalls Mediterranean serpent guardians of treasure and keepers of secret wisdom.

980. Across cultures, whether in grimoires or village games, the recurring pattern is the same: ritual creates focus, belief gives it power, and community amplifies the effect. Whether one believes in literal demons or not, the practices reveal humanity's enduring urge to reach beyond the visible world for answers, protection, or forbidden power.

981. In Japan, the Bath Game, or Darumasan, is a chilling ritual said to summon the ghost of a one-eyed woman. To begin, you must sit alone in a dark bathroom, close your eyes, and wash your hair while repeating the phrase "Darumasan fell down." Legend says this reenacts her fatal slip in the bath, after which you will sense her presence behind you. You must not turn around.

The next day, the game begins in earnest. The ghost is said to follow you everywhere, creeping closer with each passing hour. If you spot her, you can buy yourself time by shouting "Tomare!" ("Stop!"). But to end the game completely, you must cut the air with your hand and cry "Kitta!" ("I cut you loose!"). Those who forget the final step, folklore warns, may never be free — doomed to feel her just behind them, forever watching.

982. Ancient Egyptians engaged in retainer sacrifices during the earliest dynasties. At Abydos, tombs of pharaohs such as King Djer and King Aha contained servants buried with tools, possibly alive, to serve them in

the afterlife. Eventually, this practice was replaced by symbolic human figures.

983. Divination isn't about locking in the future — it's about finding clarity in the present. It reads the world as a web of signs, using tools like tarot cards, astrology charts, runes, or the I Ching to pull meaning from patterns. Some see it as a way to hear from spirits or ancestors; others say it's your own subconscious speaking in symbols. Either way, it's less about certainty and more about insight.

984. In ancient Persia, Zoroastrian fire rituals centered on sacred flames kept burning in fire temples, representing purity and the divine presence of Ahura Mazda. Priests tended these eternal fires with strict care, and worshippers honored them through offerings and prayers. While the outward practices are documented, the deeper symbolic and esoteric meanings behind the ceremonies remain partly mysterious.

985. In South Africa, one of the most striking cultural ceremonies is the Zulu Reed Dance, or uMkhosi woMhlanga. Held annually, it gathers thousands of young Zulu women who journey to the royal palace carrying tall reeds cut from riverbeds. These reeds are presented to the king as a symbolic gesture of purity, unity, and respect, reinforcing bonds between the monarchy and the people.

The ritual stretches back centuries and serves multiple purposes: it celebrates womanhood, honors chastity, and reaffirms Zulu identity in a collective display of tradition. The young women, dressed in colorful beadwork and traditional attire, dance and sing before the king and his court in a vibrant expression of cultural pride. Beyond symbolism, the ceremony also acts as a rite of passage, linking younger generations to ancestral customs and reminding them of their role within the community.

Though sometimes viewed through modern debates about gender and tradition, the Reed Dance remains a cornerstone of Zulu heritage. For participants and onlookers alike, it's both spectacle and sacred duty — a celebration of continuity where song, dance, and ritual keep centuries-old identity alive in the heart of contemporary South Africa.

986. The legend of El Silbón ("the Whistler") from the Venezuelan and Colombian llanos tells of a spectral figure whose eerie, distance-tricking whistle portends misfortune or death. Folk practices — keeping dogs close, avoiding whistling at night — reflect community caution; it's a moral tale and a nocturnal scare rolled into one.

987. Elite bloodletting could get intimate. After dragging stingray spines or obsidian through their tongues, participants sometimes entered ritual unions — joined in trance, sex, or both. Whether it was literal or symbolic varies depending on where you look, but the fusion of pain, blood, and power was the point.

988. One-Man Hide and Seek, or Hitori Kakurenbo, is a Japanese ritual game considered one of the most dangerous. A doll is stuffed with rice and personal DNA, such as fingernail clippings, then bound with red thread and stabbed after being declared "it." Believed to become possessed by a spirit, the doll is said to roam in search of the player. To survive, one must end the game properly — by spitting salt water on the doll, cutting the thread, and burning it. According to legend, those who fail vanish without a trace.

989. High, or ceremonial, magic is less about casting spells and more about transforming the self. It follows a structured, symbol-rich path toward spiritual awakening — what practitioners call the "Great Work." Rituals are carefully timed with planets, using tools like wands, swords, chalices, and pentacles, all layered with meaning. Robes are worn, and divine names are invoked. Its roots stretch through Hermeticism, Kabbalah, alchemy, and Neoplatonism, with major systems like Enochian magic, the Golden Dawn, and the Tree of Life mapping the climb from the earthly to the divine.

990. Kokkuri-san is Japan's Ouija. You draw a board, use a coin as a planchette, and call Kokkuri, a fox-spirit trickster. He answers truthfully, or not. You must never forget to dismiss him properly, or he lingers. Schools banned this game, but bans only fuel curiosity.

991. King Paimon, named in grimoires like The Lesser Key of Solomon as one of the "Four Kings of Hell," is traditionally depicted not as a destroyer but as a spirit who teaches hidden wisdom, philosophy, and the

sciences. His arrival is said to be heralded by loud music, cymbals, and noise — symbolizing a rupture of ordinary reality. Though modern pop culture, especially the film *Hereditary*, reimagines him in a darker, more gruesome light, older sources emphasize his role as a revealer of secret knowledge.

992. Among the Sateré-Mawé of Brazil, the bullet-ant glove rite marks a boy's passage into manhood. Sedated ants are woven into gloves with their stingers facing inward; initiates must endure excruciating stings while dancing through the pain — an ordeal repeated multiple times. It's an extreme, community-valued test of endurance and identity, not a spectacle for outsiders.

993. Descendants of the Mandan people preserve symbolic forms of the Okipa, a traditional vision quest that once involved suspending young men by chest piercings and dragging buffalo skulls. Full versions of the ritual largely ended due to modern legal restrictions, though its cultural meaning endures.

994. During Thaipusam in Malaysia and India, devotees prepare with weeks of fasting and meditation before walking barefoot while carrying kavadi — ornate physical burdens that symbolize penance and devotion. As an act of purification and devotion to the god Murugan, many pierce their cheeks, tongues, and backs with hooks and skewers in a display of ecstatic faith.

995. The "Nine Unknown Men" is a modern legend ascribed to Emperor Aśoka: 9 guardians, each tasked with protecting dangerous knowledge such as biological or psychological warfare. It functions as conspiracy folklore about hidden custodians of science; there's no solid historical proof, but the story persists in novels and internet lore.

996. In parts of Karnataka and Maharashtra in India parents drop their infants from rooftops into cloths held below, a centuries-old tradition that is said to bring good fortune and protection, though it understandably raises serious safety concerns today.

997. The Sacred Cenote at Chichén Itzá wasn't just a sinkhole — it was a ritual gateway. Archaeologists have found bones from men, women, and children alongside gold, jade, and other offerings, pointing to formalized

water sacrifices. Some remains suggest the victims were thrown in alive. Later colonial accounts added darker, moralized layers to the story, but those details remain debated.

998. The Mithraic Mysteries of the Roman Empire centered on the cult of Mithras, popular among soldiers. Their ceremonies took place in underground temples and often depicted Mithras slaying a bull — a symbol of renewal and fertility. Yet the deeper meaning of these rites and the reason for their secrecy remain uncertain.

999. In many ancient cultures, adultery and other "forbidden" sexual acts weren't just personal scandals — they were seen as violations of cosmic order. Punishments ranged from public humiliation to death, but how harshly the rules were applied often depended on status, gender, or politics. Some were made examples; others slipped through. Whether these laws were strictly enforced or mostly symbolic is still up for debate.

1000. In the Shang Dynasty of China, human sacrifice was both common and highly systematized. Pit sacrifices involved dismembered young men; foundation sacrifices used children and infants to sanctify buildings; and internment sacrifices buried intact young women alongside elite burials. These rituals reinforced political power and religious beliefs, and all victims were buried without personal possessions.

Thank You for Reading!

Thank you so much for joining me on this learning adventure. I hope you had fun exploring new facts, testing your knowledge, and discovering big ideas along the way.

If you enjoyed this book, I'd be very grateful if you could leave a review on Amazon. You can simply scan the QR code below to share your thoughts. Reviews help other families, teachers, and curious readers find books they'll enjoy.

Even a short review makes a big difference — and I truly appreciate your support!

See you in the next book!

Millie

www.ingramcontent.com/pod-product-compliance
Lightning Source LLC
Chambersburg PA
CBHW071204070526
44584CB00019B/2910